D1431425

Faith, Freedom, and the Future

Faith, Freedom, and the Future

Religion in American Political Culture

CHARLES W. DUNN

ROWMAN & LITTLEFIELD PUBLISHERS, INC.
Lanham • Boulder • New York • Oxford

ROWMAN & LITTLEFIELD PUBLISHERS, INC.

Published in the United States of America
by Rowman & Littlefield Publishers, Inc.
A Member of the Rowman & Littlefield Publishing Group
4720 Boston Way, Lanham, Maryland 20706
www.rowmanlittlefield.com

PO Box 317
Oxford
OX2 9RU, UK

British Library Cataloguing in Publication Information Available

Library of Congress Cataloging-in-Publication Data
   Faith, freedom, and the future : religion in american political culture /
Charles W. Dunn.
      p.   cm.
   Includes bibliographical references.
   ISBN 0-7425-2330-6 (hard : alk. paper)
   1. Christianity and politics—United States—History. I. Dunn,
Charles W.

   BR115.P7 F29 2002
   322'.1'0973—dc21

                                                            2002009695

Printed in the United States of America

♾ The paper used in this publication meets the minimum requirements of
American National Standard for Information Sciences—Permanence of Paper for
Printed Library Materials, ANSI/NISO Z39.48-1992.

Contents

Preface

No subject arouses more passionate controversy than faith and freedom. From the rise of Islam and terrorism to the demise of America's religious traditions, faith and freedom cut to the heart and soul of America and her position in the world. The issues spawned by faith and freedom spark untold controversies about our perception of history and our vision for the future. As Americans we hold countless contrary views about the nature of God and humanity and about what government should do and how. Never far from center stage during these debates are faith and freedom.

Sadly, for much of American history scholars ignored faith and freedom, considering the subject of little or no consequence. But now scholars of great stature lead the way in assessing its significance.

Recognizing the importance of faith and freedom to America's future, Grove City College titled its 125th Anniversary Lecture Series *Faith, Freedom, and the Future*. Addressing this subject from a wide variety of perspectives in this lecture series were eight internationally recognized scholars:

- James H. Billington, Librarian of Congress
- Mark A. Noll, McManis Professor of Christian Thought (Wheaton College)
- Marvin Olasky, editor of *World* magazine and Professor of Journalism (University of Texas)
- George Marsden, Francis A. McAnaney Professor of History (Notre Dame)

- Jean Bethke Elshtain, Laura Spelman Rockefeller Professor of Social and Political Ethics (University of Chicago)
- Robert P. George, McCormick Professor of Jurisprudence (Princeton)
- Michael J. Behe, Professor of Biological Sciences (Lehigh)
- George Weigel, Senior Fellow and John M. Olin Chair in Religion and American Democracy (Ethics and Public Policy Center)

This book, *Faith, Freedom, and the Future: Religion in American Political Culture*, culminates a year long examination of this vitally important subject. Just how momentous and timely are the topics addressed herein? Many people drove an hour or more to attend the lectures, including some from places as distant as Cleveland and Pittsburgh.

Many others contributed to the success of the lecture series, but particularly Grove City College president John H. Moore, who envisioned it. Meriting special appreciation for their outstanding support of the lectures are the faculty, staff, and students of the College. Of course, I must express special appreciation to Mary Carpenter, acquisitions editor at Rowman & Littlefield, for her confidence in the value of publishing *Faith, Freedom, and the Future: Religion in American Political Culture.*

Introduction

The Kaleidoscopic Dynamics of Faith and Freedom

Charles W. Dunn

As light shines into a kaleidoscope, producing a kaleidoscopic result—endless and constantly changing patterns of light—so faith and freedom produce a kaleidoscopic display of American values. While American values appear in kaleidoscopic patterns, focusing on the product of the kaleidoscope presents a daunting task—much like piecing together a mosaic of fragments without benefit of the artist's vision of the mosaic. Since the endless and constantly changing patterns of light are not a cause but a result, profit rests in an examination of the causes and consequences of kaleidoscopic values in American society.

First, though, how important are values in society? According to sociologist Robert N. Bellah, widely shared values or moral understandings enable a society to maintain cohesion.

> . . . any coherent and viable society rests on a common set of moral understandings about good and bad, right and wrong, in the realm of individual and social action. It is almost as widely held that these common moral understandings must also rest in turn upon a common set of religious understandings that provide a picture of the universe in terms of

CHARLES W. DUNN, Dean of the School of Arts & Letters at Grove City College and former Chairman of the United States J. William Fulbright Board, includes the following among his ten books: *The Scarlet Thread of Scandal: Morality and the American Presidency, The Conservative Tradition in America, American Government in Comparative Perspective, American Democracy Debated,* and *The Future of the American Presidency.*

which the moral understandings make sense. Such moral and religious understandings produce both a basic cultural legitimation for a society which is viewed as at least approximately in accord with them, and a standard of judgment for the criticism of society that is seen as deviating too far from them.[1]

Kaleidoscopically, moral understandings in America have moved along a continuum from uniformity to diversity and from simplicity to complexity. To illustrate, consider how far Harvard University has traveled from its origins. When founded, Harvard's charter expressed this purpose: "Everyone shall consider the main end of his life to know God and Jesus Christ which is eternal life."[2] No longer representative of the institution it governs, this charter demonstrates the conflict wrought by the kaleidoscopic nature of America's moral understandings.

When Alexander Solzhenitsyn delivered his controversial commencement address at Harvard University in 1978, he highlighted the conflict between the historic Christian faith and the emerging faith of humanism: "The humanistic way of thinking . . . started Western civilization on the dangerous trend of worshipping man and his material needs."[3] Echoing Solzhenitsyn's analysis, although opposed to his position, John Dunphy states that "The classroom . . . will become an arena of conflict between the old and the new—the rotting corpse of Christianity . . . and the new faith of humanism."[4] Stark contrast and strident conflict now mark America's moral understandings.

In legislative halls and courtroom chambers, the issues of faith and freedom divide Americans, producing a kaleidoscopic array of competing values and moral understandings.

- Should parents receive vouchers to send their children to private and religious schools?
- Should public schools teach both creation and evolution?
- What financial aid, if any, should organizations such as the Salvation Army receive from the government?
- To what extent, if at all, should public schools allow religious meetings and practices such as Bible clubs and prayers before athletic events and at commencements?
- Should religious organizations have the freedom to determine

their own standards for employees, including the right to prohibit the employment of homosexuals?

- What roles, if any, should religious leaders play in politics?
- Should public schools allow a moment of silence at the beginning of the school day?
- What limits, if any, should the government place on abortion?
- Should nativity scenes, the Ten Commandments, and other religious statements and traditions appear on public property?
- Should the government prohibit human cloning?

While Americans face deep divisions today about their moral understandings of right and wrong, good and bad, in earlier eras these divisions were either nonexistent or masked or only partially revealed.

Faith and Freedom in American History

Framers of the American Constitution, steeped in various forms of Protestantism, could hardly have understood today's call by civil libertarians to divorce religion from public life. Over a century ago, in 1892, in what today we would regard as an incredible and an inconceivable decision, *Church of the Holy Trinity v. U.S.* (143 U.S. 471), the U.S. Supreme Court unanimously declared that "we find everywhere a clear recognition of the same truth . . . that this is a Christian nation." To reach this decision, the court reviewed the history of the colonial charters, the Declaration of Independence, the U.S. Constitution, the state constitutions, and other sources, whereupon it stated:

> There is no dissonance in these declarations. There is a universal language pervading them all, having one meaning: they affirm and reaffirm that this is a religious nation. These are not individual sayings, declarations of private persons: they are organic utterances; they speak the voice of the entire people. While because of a general recognition of this truth the question has seldom been presented to the courts, yet we find that . . . "Christianity, general Christianity, is and always has been a part of the common law."

Today many Americans not only concur with the court's opinion in

Church of the Holy Trinity v. U.S. (143 U.S. 471), but they also work to re-claim its legacy, which Justice David J. Brewer articulated at Harvard College in 1905: "This Republic is classified among the Christian nations of the world. It was so formally declared by the Supreme Court of the United States . . . in the case of *Holy Trinity Church v. United States.*"[5]

The mainstream of today's secular society, however, regards their aspirations and Justice Brewer's thinking as fanciful and wishful, at best. And some offer counterclaims to the proposition that America began as a Christian nation, contending that *The Federalist Papers,* the fundamental explanation of the government established, contains no references either to God or to the Bible; that such leading architects of America's founding as Thomas Jefferson and James Madison generally avoided biblical references in their writings; that no references to deity appear in the U.S. Constitution and only a few in the Declaration of Independence; and that the founders emphasized "natural law" rather than "divine law," believing that the rights of man inhere in his being, not because he is God's creation.[6]

Nonetheless, the two sides, represented by many organizations arrayed in battle formation, fight to influence the future of America's moral understandings in large measure because they differ in their interpretations of the past and in their desires for the future. The legions of organizations include the visible and influential People for the American Way and the American Civil Liberties Union on one side and Focus on the Family and the Traditional Values Coalition on the other. Their representatives actively struggle for advantage on many fronts—the courts, the Congress, the Executive, the media, political parties, and state and local government.

While the principles of "no establishment" and "free exercise" in the First Amendment may guide debates on these issues, they do not govern their resolution. When the founders stated, "Congress shall make no law respecting an establishment of religion nor prohibiting the free exercise thereof," they left to succeeding generations the responsibility of interpreting and applying these two principles. Like putty that never hardens, succeeding generations have reinterpreted and reapplied these principles in many and often conflicting ways. For example, where prayer and Bible reading were once commonplace in public settings throughout America, they are now increasingly absent as the "no establishment" clause has trumped the "free exercise" clause on many issues pertaining to faith and freedom.

Americans today cope with divisions that the founders could not have anticipated. Influenced primarily by the various forms of Protestantism of their time, the founders could not have understood how economic, political, religious, and social changes would alter the application of the Constitution's First Amendment. In the founders' America, several states had established churches, and throughout the burgeoning nation many other strong and visible links connected the sacred and the secular in public life. Not only would the founders find incomprehensible today's demands to annul the commingling of faith and freedom in public life, but also they could not have foreseen the effects of education, industrialization, and immigration in the nineteenth century.

During the 1800s such social scientists as Marx forecast the demise of religious faith in industrial society, while proponents of modernization theories contended that the forces of education, industrialization, and urbanization would make religious faith obsolete. Marxian analysis declared that religious faith, the opiate of the masses, would become obsolete as people rose up to throw off the shackles of elitist economic tyranny perpetrated by religious dogma about acceptance of their servant status. Proponents of modernization theories forecast that as people became better educated and moved from farm to city, they would no longer need the crutch of religious faith, but rather would recognize that their problems could be solved by higher education and advances in science.

But contrary to these predictions the issues of faith and freedom continue to exercise dramatic influence throughout the world and in America. Most Americans, for example, continue to hold traditional religious beliefs and to maintain an allegiance to a church, synagogue, or other religious organization. Issues of faith and freedom have also prompted many Americans to enter the political arena, seeking to influence the outcome of public debates on such diverse issues as war and peace, poverty, and personal morality.

Only in the last twenty-five years or so have scholars begun to investigate seriously the impact of faith and freedom on American society. Their failure created a major vacuum in our understanding of how faith and freedom influence America's increasingly complex values and moral understandings. Why this oversight? According to Seymour Martin Lipset and Peter L. Benson, scholars have only reluctantly studied the issues of faith and freedom, because the mainstream of academia has stigmatized their study, considering these issues either less important than other subjects or perhaps even outside the pale of legitimate scholarship.[7] In 1977 Peter L. Berger and Richard John Neuhaus contended: "there is a profoundly anti-democratic prejudice in public policy discourse that ignores the role of religious institutions in the lives of most Americans."[8] Adding to this point, Michael Novak noted in 1980: "There is a hidden religious power base in American culture, which our secular biases prevent many of us from noticing."[9] But since the early 1980s, the walls of reservation and opposition to serious scholarly inquiry have collapsed as waves of articles and books, research institutes and doctoral programs began to address the issues of faith and freedom.

So where are we now? Although most Americans profess religious faith, they live in a society that has abandoned many public manifestations of faith. Religious and political leaders disagree on what to do about the situation, and scholars have only recently begun to clarify the role of faith and freedom in American society. Meanwhile, competing constitutional principles often exacerbate rather than resolve the issues. The result: a kaleidoscopic array of competing values and moral understandings.

Pluralism and the American Kaleidoscope

Always at least somewhat heterogeneous, America has accommodated and adjusted to the competing interests of a variety of ethnic groups, races, classes, and religious faiths. But does pluralism, which allows these competing interests to coexist, leave society devoid of moral understandings and a sense of direction? The answer to this important question rests in an examination of pluralism from the founding until now.

PROTESTANT DOMINANCE: THE COLONIAL ERA

Protestant Christianity dominated American society in colonial times. French Roman Catholic writer Alexis de Tocqueville concluded that "The greatest part of British America was peopled by men who, after having shaken off the authority of the Pope, acknowledged no other religious supremacy: They brought with them into the New World a form of Christianity which I cannot better describe than by styling it a democratic and republican religion."[10] Harvard University historian Samuel Eliot Morison confirmed Tocqueville's conclusion:

> Puritanism was a cutting edge which hewed liberty, democracy, humanitarianism, and universal education out of the black forest of feudal Europe and the American wilderness.
>
> Puritan doctrine taught each person to consider himself a significant if sinful unit to whom God had given a particular place and duty, and

that he must help his fellow men. Puritanism is an American heritage to be grateful for and not to be sneered at because it required everyone to attend divine worship and maintained a strict code of moral ethics.[11]

Colonial and college charters in this era exhibited the marks of Protestant, and particularly Puritan, Christianity. The Fundamental Orders of Connecticut (1638–1639) boldly declared its goal: "to maintain and pursue the liberty and purity of the gospel of our Lord Jesus which we now profess, as also the discipline of the Churches, which according to the truth of the said gospel is now practiced amongst us." Similarly the Yale charter stated this objective: "to propagate . . . the blessed reformed Protestant religion in the purity of its order and worship."[12]

Common to many colonies were established churches, Puritan or Congregational churches in the North and Anglican in the South. Among the thirteen colonies, seven had established churches—Connecticut, Georgia, Maryland, Massachusetts, New Hampshire, South Carolina, and Virginia. Six did not—Delaware, New Jersey, New York, North Carolina, Pennsylvania, and Rhode Island. Also widespread among the colonial charters and early state constitutions were religious tests for holding office. Pennsylvania, the most pluralistically tolerant state, required in 1776 that legislators take this oath: "I do believe in one God, the creator and governor of the universe, the rewarder of the good and the punisher of the wicked. And I do acknowledge the Scriptures of the Old and New Testament to be given by Divine inspiration." The Delaware Constitution mandated that officeholders take this pledge in 1776: "I do profess faith in God the Father, and in Jesus Christ His only Son, and in the Holy Ghost, one God, blessed for evermore; and I do acknowledge the holy scriptures of the Old and New Testament to be given by divine inspiration."[13]

While church membership in the colonies was low, requirements for membership were high, generating far higher figures for church attendance than for church membership. Religious influence pervaded colonial society. Tiny Jewish and Roman Catholic populations ensured that Protestant Christianity dominated, but not monolithically. Pluralism rather than unity typified Protestant Christianity. Found among the colonies were Baptists and Moravians, Quakers and Presbyterians, Mennonites and Congregationalists, Anglicans and Methodists, and others. Meanwhile, the deism of Thomas Jefferson and Benjamin Franklin contributed yet another dimension. Although lacking a large number of adherents, deism's influence extended far beyond what its numbers would suggest. Generally well-educated and often well-placed politically, deists exercised considerable power and prestige. Deists and Protestants disagreed on many religious doctrines, such as the divine inspiration of the Bible and the deity and virgin birth of Jesus Christ, but they agreed on two exceedingly important issues of faith and freedom: opposition to the establishment of a national church and support for individual freedom.

FORESHADOWING CHANGE: THE PRE–CIVIL WAR ERA

Although the big picture changed little between the founding and the Civil War, increases in religious diversity and immigration foreshadowed major changes and challenges. Protestant Christianity remained dominant, but Unitarianism, Transcendentalism and various utopian faiths presented doctrinal challenges. Unitarianism denied the deity of Christ and other cardinal Protestant doctrines, Transcendentalism taught that everyone has the spark of divinity and that no one is born into sin, and utopian religions desired to establish perfect communities. Waves of new immigrants, particularly Jews from Germany and Roman Catholics from Ireland, created the potential for even more significant challenges to the supremacy of Protestant Christianity. Also during this era, church membership increased as membership standards decreased.

Exercising cautious activism during this period, Protestant Christianity in the main left politics to politicians except on a few major issues. Protestant activists stood against slavery in the North, advocated prohibition, called for Sunday blue laws and espoused reform of prisons and mental institutions. Alexis de Tocqueville aptly described Protestant Christianity's dominant role in society: "In the United States religion exercises little influence upon the laws and upon the details of public opinion; but it directs the customs of the community, and by regulating domestic life, it regulates the state."[14] Facing only minimal challenges to its dominance, Protestant Christianity had little need to assert itself in politics. Tensions between Protestant Christianity and other faiths that emerged during the twentieth century owe their origins to this period, as do the origins of a less sacred and a more secular society. In 1801 Yale University President Timothy Dwight foreshadowed the demise of Protestant Christianity's domain:

You must take your side. There can be no halting between two opinions. . . . Between them and you there is, there can be, no natural, real, or lasting harmony. . . . Will you imbibe their principles? Will you copy their practices? Will you teach your children, that death is an eternal sleep; that the end sanctifies the means? that moral obligation is a dream? Religion a farce? . . . Will you burn your Bibles? Will you crucify anew your Redeemer? Will you deny your God?[15]

PRELUDE TO CHANGE: THE CIVIL WAR TO WORLD WAR II

The forces that ultimately challenged and toppled Protestant Christianity's cultural dominance gained momentum from the Civil War to World War II. Thirteen million Roman Catholics and Jews immigrated to the United States between 1900 and 1914, sharp theological cleavages created cracks in mainstream Protestant Christianity, and pluralism made significant strides in American society. Since Catholics and Jews remained a distinct minority during this era, Protestant Christianity remained dominant, but not without feeling their presence. Responding to the waves of new immigrants with distinctly different faiths, Protestants attempted to reduce immigration, increased their emphasis on Bible reading in the public schools, and promoted citywide revival meetings, stressing personal salvation and social reform, including prohibition.

Internal divisions eroded the power of Protestant Christianity even further. Besides the advent of new holiness and Pentecostal movements, which created more Protestant denominations, Protestant Christianity ruptured theologically between the historically dominant conservative Protestants and the emerging liberal Protestants. Two of the most widely publicized battles occurred among Presbyterians at Princeton University and Seminary and in the northern Presbyterian denomination. Liberal Protestants won both. Inspired by such novel theological ideas as the social gospel and neo-orthodoxy, liberal Protestants increased their political activism, aspiring to usher in the kingdom of God on earth through the lever of governmental social action. The Methodist Social Creed of 1908 represented one of the earliest statements of liberal social gospel theology. Neo-orthodox theology also influenced liberal Protestantism by redefining and modernizing such traditional conservative Protestant theological terms as sin, heaven, hell, righteousness, and salvation, making the terms more palatable to an increasingly secular America. Although conservative Protestants fought back, they lost most of the battles for control of mainstream religious denominations and colleges, including Presbyterian, Episcopalian, Methodist, and others.

CONFLICT AND TRANSFORMATION: WORLD WAR II TO THE PRESENT

On the eve of this era, the death of prohibition foreshadowed a dramatic decline in the dominance of conservative Protestant Christianity. The demise of several decades-old traditions illustrate this decline, including Sunday closing laws, Bible reading and prayer in the schools, nativity scenes on public property, sermons by clergy at baccalaureate services, and prayers before athletic events at public schools. Combined with the legalization of abortion and the legal recognition of homosexuality, conservative Protestant Christianity found itself on the defensive on many fronts.

Using their enlarged and better educated numbers, Roman Catholics helped to elect the first Roman Catholic president in 1960 and to secure financial aid for parochial schools in the 1965 Elementary and Secondary Education Act. Averse to the dictates of Protestant culture on such issues as opposition to alcohol consumption and gambling and observance of Sunday as the Lord's Day, Roman Catholics and Jews accelerated the decline of the historically dominant conservative Protestant culture.

Among liberal Protestants, Jews, and some Roman Catholics, the 1960s enabled them to participate in the American civil rights movement, working closely with its best-known leader, Baptist preacher Martin Luther King, Jr. Elsewhere in the 1960s the American Civil Liberties Union, together with many liberal Protestant and Jewish members, successfully challenged the cherished traditions of America's conservative Protestant culture in the courts on such issues as prayer and Bible reading in the schools.

Opposed to the passing of America's historic Protestant culture, conservatives counterattacked. During the late 1970s, conservative leaders and interest groups began massive organizational efforts to challenge liberal Protestantism and the demise of America's historic Protestant culture. In addition to their organizational and media efforts on television and radio, they started Christian schools in large numbers to oppose the secularizing influences of the public school system.

But conservative Protestants were not alone in their feeling of alienation from American culture. Also during the 1970s, conservative Roman Catholics sensed challenges to their own doctrinal beliefs on such issues as abortion and homosexuality. By the late 1970s and early 1980s conservative Protestants and Catholics had begun to fight for common interests, joining in 1980 to help elect Ronald Reagan as president. White Protestants in the South and conservative Catholics in the North migrated from the Democratic Party to the Republican Party. On the interest-group scene many conservative religious groups formed, including the Catholic-inspired Eagle Forum and the Protestant-inspired Moral Majority and Christian Coalition, to challenge the National Council of Churches and other liberal religious interest groups.

Conservative Protestant resurgence, largely the product of fundamental, charismatic, Pentecostal, and evangelical denominations and organizations, paved the way for rapid church growth, including the megachurch movement, which spawned scores of churches into the thousands of members. The fastest growing churches included independents, fundamental Baptists, Southern Baptists, charismatics and Pentecostals, such as the Assemblies of God and Church of God, and Mormons, although historically they are not considered a Christian denomination.

The Roman Catholic Church, divided between conservatives and liberals by the changes of Vatican II during the 1960s, experienced its own conservative growth under the leadership of a conservative pontiff, John Paul II. Conservative religious orders, such as the Legionnaires of Christ, realized dramatic growth, while liberal religious orders, such as the Jesuits, suffered large losses. The charismatic movement also penetrated the Roman Catholic community. As Catholics dramatically increased their influence economically, politically, and socially in American society, they set the stage for the "Catholic Moment" in America, an opportunity to eclipse Protestant cultural dominance.

Since the 1960s, conservative and orthodox branches of Judaism have enjoyed significant growth as more Jews began to take historic Judaism seriously. Additionally Jews discovered new allies among fundamental and evangelical Protestants and conservative Catholics, whose biblical views inspired their support for Israel. Despite Republican Party entreaties, however, Jews have generally remained loyal to the Democratic Party. Republicans might have had more success in these appeals had they not offended Jews by their highly visible cultivation of conservative Protestants and Catholics.

The Black community, overwhelmingly Protestant, shifted its allegiance from the Republican Party of Abraham Lincoln to the Democratic Party of Franklin D. Roosevelt during the 1930s, where they remain, usually giving 90 percent or so of their votes to Democratic Party presidential candidates. The Civil Rights and Voting Rights Acts of 1964 and 1965 and Jesse Jackson's presidential candidacies in 1984 and 1988 solidified Black allegiance to the Democratic Party. Jackson's close ties to the American Muslim community, however, alienated many Jews who had vigorously supported the civil rights movement. Ironically, the civil rights movement had depended greatly on Jewish financial, intellectual, and political assistance.

Today, with the rapid rise of Islam in America, American pluralism has become more pronounced. Once known as the church of American presidents, the Episcopal Church now has fewer adherents than Islam. Although Muslims have not yet established a significant political presence, they have a sufficient population to begin influencing American values and moral understandings. Yet another rapidly growing movement contributing to America's kaleidoscopic values and moral understandings, the New Age movement poses even more challenges to the cultural influences of both Protestants and Catholics, who emphasize the importance of God in creation and human existence. The New Age movement stresses that life exists separately from the external reference point of God and revealed Scripture. Manifested in spiritual, pagan, occult, and metaphysical writings, New Age books possess a large presence on the bookshelves of major trade bookstores.

As America became more pluralistic, the American kaleidoscope became more complex, producing an ever-greater variety of values and moral understandings. First, immigration contributed to pluralism as Catholics, Jews, and other immigrant groups challenged Protestantism's dominance. Second, division within Protestantism, especially the advent of liberal Protestantism and the increasing number of Protestant denominations, added impetus to pluralism. Third, the power of traditional Protestantism gradually receded under the challenges brought about by immigration and division. Fourth, whether the current resurgence of conservative Protestantism is anything other than a brief reassertion of a lost past remains an open question. Fifth, likewise whether Catholicism can eclipse Protestantism's influence, making this the Catholic Moment in America, remains problematic. Sixth, the rise of Islam and the New Age movement illustrate other pluralist forces contributing to diversity and division among American values and moral understandings. The modern era not only climaxes a long history of changes in American values and moral understandings, but it also points to the importance of discerning the significance of faith and freedom.

The Kaleidoscope of Faith and Freedom

Competing claims and tensions about values and moral understandings in America magnify an important question: To what extent, if at all, should faith and freedom influence public life and democratic decision-making in America? Two conflicting answers with many variations in between illustrate the complexity this question poses.

First, some believe that human beings do not need either a supreme being or a book of sacred Scripture to achieve self-fulfillment and a cohesive society. Allied with them, others fear that linking politics and religion, even if it favors their own beliefs, would deny religious freedom to others. Second, opposite this position, another holds that without a firm moral foundation emanating from deity and sacred Scripture, society's foundations will crumble. Understandably those taking this position desire to apply the precepts and tenets of deity and sacred Scripture to such issues as education, abortion, sexual practices, clergy in politics, and so on.

These two positions—poles apart in their interpretations of America's past, their perceptions of the present, and their visions for the future—hold contrary views about the nature of God and humanity and about what government should do and how. The dramatic divisions between the two positions highlight important questions about public policy.

- What standards should guide the making of public policy in America?
- What standards should direct an assessment of the success of public policy decisions?
- Should the will or opinion of the people serve as the sole determinant of public policy and as an evaluation of its success?
- Should an external reference point, namely deity and sacred Scripture, serve as the ultimate authority?
- If society and government use an external reference point in making and evaluating public policy, who should determine and apply it?

Many maintain that American democracy should use ethical and moral measurements of divine origin as the ultimate guide in making these decisions and judgments. But what are those measurements? In the largely conservative Protestant culture of America's past, society and government could more easily reach consensus on this question. Ironically, in contemporary America such divergent voices as Martin Luther King, and Jesse Jackson on one hand and Jerry Falwell and Pat Robertson on the other have claimed to know what those measurements are.

Deep divisions regarding the propriety of our divergent values and moral understandings tear us apart. Religion, once the glue bonding society together, now severs that bond. Competing on the same political terrain with nonreligious interests while trying to influence public policy, religious interests no longer function as they once did. As Alexis de Tocqueville observed in the early 1800s, religion regulated the state by controlling community customs and directing domestic life.[16] In today's pluralistic democracy, religious interests occupy a role no more exalted than any other interest. Secularization in American politics and society has generally lowered religious interests to merely another competing political force.

The issues are genuine. The emotions are passionate. The solutions are doubtful. In the courtroom and on the campaign trail, combatants on the issues of faith and freedom play for high stakes. Although religion influences politics, politics moves religion as a pawn on the political chessboard. No longer does religion play its historic role in American politics.

Notes

1. Robert N. Bellah, *The Broken Covenant: American Civil Religion in Time of Trial* (New York: Seabury Press, 1975), ix.

2. Michael Novak, *Choosing Our King* (New York: Macmillan, 1974), 114.

3. Alexander L. Solzhenitsyn, *A World Split Apart* (New York: Harper & Row, 1978), 49, 53.

4. John Dunphy, "A Religion for a New Age," *The Humanist* 43 (January/February 1983): 26.

5. Norman De Jong, "The First Amendment: A Comparison of Nineteenth and Twentieth Century Supreme Court Interpretations," *Journal of Political Science* 16 (Spring 1988), 69.

6. Charles W. Dunn, *American Political Theology: Historical Perspective and Theoretical Analysis* (New York: Praeger, 1984), 10–28.

7. Robert Lee and Martin E. Marty, eds., *Religion and Social Conflict* (New York: Oxford University Press, 1964), 70; Peter L. Benson, "Religion on Capitol Hill," *Psychology Today* 15 (1981): 57.

8. Peter L. Berger and Richard John Neuhaus, *To Empower the People* (Washington, D.C.: American Enterprise Institute, 1977), 28.

9. Michael Novak, *Choosing Presidents: Symbols of Leadership* (New Brunswick, NJ: Transaction, 1992), 337.

10. Alexis de Tocqueville, *Democracy in America* (New York: Vintage Books, 1954), 311.

11. Charles L. Wallis, ed., *Our American Heritage* (New York: Harper & Row, 1970), 26.

12. For this and a selection of other founding documents, see Charles W. Dunn, *The Conservative Tradition in America* (Lanham, Md: Rowman & Littlefield, 1996), 132–35. See also Benjamin Perley Poore, ed., *The Federal and State Constitutions, Colonial Charters and Other Organic Laws of the United States* (Washington, D.C.: U.S. Government Printing Office, 1877).

13. Dunn, *The Conservative Tradition in America,* 132–35.

14. Alexis de Tocqueville as cited in Robert S. Alley, *So Help Me God* (Richmond, Va: John Knox Press, 1972), 21.

15. Timothy Dwight, *A Discourse on Some Events of the Last Century* (New Haven, Conn.: 1801), as quoted in Charles W. Dunn, *American Political Theology,* 25, 26.

16. Tocqueville as quoted in Alley, *So Help Me God.*

Faith, Freedom, and
the Future

Chapter One

Christianity and History

James H. Billington

I would like to discuss an impossibly ambitious, even arrogant agenda: basically to describe briefly Christianity as a unitary whole in history and to suggest that a Christian perspective is important for understanding the greatest political event of the late twentieth century, the collapse of Soviet Communism, and perhaps also for facing terrorism in the first great conflict of the twenty-first century.

Christian affirmation in the Nicene Creed begins with the belief in God the Father almighty maker of heaven and earth and of all things visible and invisible. It then tells the story of Jesus, suggesting that the human story is central to all of that creation, yet is centered on a particular time, and place, and person. The frame in the Bible is cosmic from Genesis at the beginning to Revelation at the end, but the pictures within that frame are microscopic. Those pictures focus on a provincial carpenter who died long ago and on a subsequent host of mostly ordinary people, alive and dead, who shared little in common except perhaps an occasional meal of bread and wine. Their names, let alone their stories, are rarely mentioned in the media or in the classroom and are mostly known only to God *in pectoris,* as the pope always says, within the heart.

JAMES H. BILLINGTON, Librarian of Congress, includes among his many books *The Icon and the Axe, Fire in the Minds of Men, Russia Transformed,* and *The Face of Russia.* He has served as Chairman of the U.S. J. William Fulbright Foreign Scholarship Board and as the Director of the Woodrow Wilson International Center for Scholars.

Success of Christianity

What is the essence of this strange faith currently of two billion people reaching into every section of the human family? This faith has in various ways stirred up the world in the last two thousand years, years that in fact are measured by its founder. It is something within those who in some way try to live their way into the founder's story praying for a father's guidance into a kingdom unlike any other, yet findable wherever two or three are gathered together in his name. Those who affirm this faith find hope through sacraments and through communities unified sometimes by an apostolically based priesthood, at other times by biblically based preaching and witness. Christianity offers a perfectionist's ideal to a relativistic world. It is spread more by example than by argument. Jesus did not answer when Pilate asked him, "What is truth?" For in the words of the great Jewish philosopher Franz Rosenzweig, "Truth is a noun only for God, for us it is always a verb," and it has to be an active not a passive verb, as Saint Paul reminded us in one of the great passages cherished by Christians through the ages. Paul was perhaps as convinced as anyone in history of the truth of Christianity, yet in his epistle to the philosophically sophisticated Corinthians he confessed that we see through a glass, only darkly. Corinth was one of the most cosmopolitan cities of classical antiquity. Paul saw that very diversity as an asset rather than a liability, and he likened those who spoke narrowly to only some small segment of that city to the speech of a child before he puts away childish things. He ends, of course, with the affirmation of three surpassing virtues: faith, hope, and love. And the greatest of these was love, the virtue with the most direct imperative to action, to the active verb.

The inner truth of Christianity is perhaps better suggested by artists and poets than by philosophers and theologians. Take for instance the most perplexing of all core Christian beliefs, belief in the Trinity. It was best expressed almost simultaneously in the Middle Ages by two very different artists who never knew each other: in the East by the last painting made by the greatest of all icon painters, Andrei Rublev, and in the West, in the beatific vision in the final canto of Dante's *Divine Comedy*. Up until their time, Christianity had been almost exclusively a Mediterranean and European religion. But after the fall of Constantinople and of the Eastern Christian Empire in 1453, a new age of exploration opened up global horizons for the faith as Christianity became the dominant, at least nominal, credo of the northern and western hemispheres, but not of the southern and eastern parts of the dominant Afro-Eurasian heartland. It particularly failed to penetrate the two oldest and most populous civilizations of the world in India and China.

Christianity never succeeded in spreading very far south or east from its original Mediterranean bases, though the Coptic, Ethiopian, Georgian, Armenian, Syrian, and Malibar Indian churches still give witness today to ancient lineages and glorious liturgies of which Western Christendom and the scholarly world in general both remain disgracefully ignorant. European Christianity historically had a strained relationship with the two other Abrahamic monotheisms that were also born in the borderland between Asia and Africa and were theologically related to Christianity: Judaism and Islam. Most of the Christian Bible is the story of the Jews, a small people who believed in one God against an ancient world that affirmed many deities. This people believed that God had chosen them to realize righteousness in time rather than merely to extend power in space, as other leaders of antiquity generally sought to do. Christianity grew out of Judaism, and the two shared a common persecution under the Roman Empire; but institutional Christianity became linked with the institutional power of empire in the fourth century and with the multiple national powers that arose in Europe beginning in the sixteenth century.

In search of a modern secular ideology that could legitimize the new national states that emerged everywhere in Europe in the nineteenth century, European Christian leaders took from their Jewish forebears the idea of a chosen people. Nationalism became a kind of secular religion and a new kind of secular anti-Semitism supplanted, even as it built on in some ways, an earlier theological anti-Judaism. Underappreciation of the majesty of the Jewish Bible was in a sense preprogrammed by the doctrinal tendency of the early church fathers to read the Old Testament almost entirely as a prefiguration of the New Testament. But I would suggest and contend that modern anti-Semitism, as its very name suggests, owes more to a neo-pagan racism than to preexistent theological antagonisms. Collectivist secular ideologies had an unrecognized need for collective blood sacrifice. Along with the tendency of the European world to use the Jews as internal scapegoats has come the tendency to see Muslims as external enemies. Even educated elites generally are unaware that classical science and philosophy were preserved and transmitted to Europe far more through medieval Muslims in twelfth-century Spain than through renaissance Christians in fourteenth-century Italy. The sad fact is that the basic Western Christian understanding of Islam has not advanced significantly beyond that of our crusading ancestors.

Division in Christianity

The defection of North European Christians into Protestantism in the early modern era and the counterattack of Mediterranean Catholicism soon led to violent conflicts, generally known as the religious wars. Arguments required armies and created by the seventeenth century what I would contend was in fact the first truly world war. It unfolded like a grand fugue, which was, of course, the dominant musical form of the age of the Baroque. It began in the East with a war between Protestant Sweden and Catholic Poland that spilled over into Orthodox Russia, creating what Russians call their Time of Troubles at the beginning of the seventeenth century—*smutnoe vremia* being better translated as time of storms, a stormy time.

And the storm continued. No sooner had this conflict ended with a treaty in 1618 than even more violent and protracted warfare broke out in central Europe, a conflict the Germans called by the name Thirty Years War. In 1648, the year that this war ended with the Treaty of Westphalia, a final spasm of violence produced in Ukraine the largest single massacre of the Jews prior to the Holocaust, followed by the bloodiest war of the century between Russia and Poland, the large-scale return of the Black Plague, and unprecedented starvation precisely in the most fertile plains in Europe. This period is known in Polish and Ukrainian as *potop,* the flood; in Hebrew as *yeven metzulah,* the abyss of despair; and in Swedish and Finnish as *stor umfreden,* the great hate.

Meanwhile, on the maritime northwestern frontier of Europe, the two most innovative and entrepreneurial of the Protestant states, England and Holland, turned naval warfare against each other everywhere from New York to the East Indies. And in southwest Europe the two greatest Catholic monarchies, France and Spain, began fighting each other in a long war that ended only with the Treaty of the Pyrenees in 1659. This spreading polyphony of violence and conflict seemed to be moving toward an apocalyptical end, from the fifth-monarchy men in England at the end of its civil war to Old Believers in Russia at the end of its prolonged troubles. For the first time since Jesus, a Jewish prophet, Shabbtai Zvi, gained a large following for his claim to be the Messiah, and both the ultra-orthodox Christian Old Believers and the Sabbatian Jews expected the end of the world in the same year, 1666. The Old Believers moved out into the virgin forests of the East, often burning themselves rather than accepting the authority of the new secular state that had triumphed everywhere in Europe by the end of the seventeenth century.

The new secular authorities that emerged from the wreckage of the religious wars domesticated Christianity by creating established churches in their domains as subordinate structures of the state. Balance of power was generally maintained between the five dominant, nominally Christian, states of Europe until the outbreak of another world war in 1914. Despite the ideological disruptions of the French Revolution and the material transformations of the Industrial Revolution, peace generally prevailed well into the nineteenth century. Monarchs still reigned with bishops of their particular denomination at their side, with French-speaking diplomats and Latin-speaking academics at their service, with Jewish doctors generally on call, and with lower-class mercenary soldiers fighting their wars under German-speaking officers.

The Napoleonic conquest that metastasized out from the militarization of the French Revolution severely challenged the tacit agreement that there should be limits to any state's territorial claims within Europe. But French Revolutionary ideas were largely contained and the balance of power restored and sustained until the first of the two great communication revolutions of the modern world exploded in Europe during the 1840s: the simultaneous onset of the telegraph, the first form of instantaneous transborder communication, along with the high-speed printing press and the railroad. The main human result was not better international understanding, as sunny optimists predicted then, but rather a rapid serial convulsion of the most violent nationalistic upheavals in 1848 since the religious wars. Far from being harbingers of freedom, these unsuccessful revolutions helped unwittingly create even more centralized and intrusive national states. The Germany of Bismarck rather than of the poet Heine, the Italy of Cavour rather than of Garibaldi, and a new type of democratic demagogue in Napoleon III. He was the first political leader anywhere in the world to be elected by universal male suffrage and to rule by style and symbol and by co-opting every idea in sight without believing in any of them. The new mass media that emerged in the late nineteenth century began replacing moral criteria with aesthetic criteria for assessing public figures.

Despite rising anarchist and labor violence, European nation-states succeeded in establishing a monopoly on violence within their borders, but they never created any system of preventing violence among and between states. During the century of general European peace between the end of the Napoleonic Wars in 1815 and the outbreak of World War I in 1914, the two bloodiest events on the planet occurred outside of Europe: the Taiping Rebellion in China and the Civil War in the United States. Both events were dominated by unusual leaders, each of whom was deeply infused with Christian ideas that are hard to relate to any single denomination. The charismatic Hung Hsiu-ch'uan, the first in a long line of leaders of anti-Western movements in China, considered himself the younger brother of Christ. Abraham Lincoln, the man who brought unity and a new birth of freedom to America, did so largely through the haunting biblical prose of his Gettysburg and Second Inaugural addresses. Both men met violent ends within a few months of each other in the 1860s, and the illusion that secular progress had tamed the beast in man ended with World War I fifty years later. National borders became bloody trenches, the youth of rival states slaughtered one another, and the social-political conflict that followed swept away the three great multi-ethnic empires on the eastern periphery of Europe: the Austrian, the Russian, and the Ottoman. In the latter occurred the first genocide of the twentieth century, the Armenian Massacre of 1915, of which Hitler once said, "Whoever remembers Armenia?"

Islam and Christianity

There had been in the Islamic world of West Asia during the early modern period a certain balance of power among the five principal Muslim states that paralleled in some way the balance of power among the states of Christian Europe. And as the Ottoman Empire that bridged Europe and Asia began to disintegrate, the Muslim majority unleashed a virtual holocaust on one of the most ancient of all Christian civilizations in Armenia. Ancient antagonisms resurfaced in the consciousness of the West. The massacre of Gordon's army at Khartoum in the Sudan and novels such as *Chitral* and *Beau Geste* describing Christian outposts being overrun by

Muslim attackers gave late Victorian optimism an apocalyptic view of a Christian Europe doomed ultimately to perish at the hands of a hostile, essentially Muslim, Afro-Asian population.

Totalitarianism and Christianity

The horror of World War I led to the creation of a new kind of pagan state in Germany and Russia—one deifying race, the other class. Russia defeated Germany in World War II, in which total fatalities climbed to a level that probably exceeded that of all preceding European wars throughout the second millennium. But the carnage had only begun, with the Holocaust of European Jews followed by waves of violent wars and revolutions in Asia and Africa, and a new form of genocide in Communist empires directed against one's own people. In Soviet Russia it was the Great Purges of the 1930s, echoed in Eastern Europe in the postwar purges, and then in Ethiopia and Cambodia. Unprecedented and often unacknowledged bloodshed accompanied the spread of the world's first political system explicitly devoted to the elimination of all religious belief.

Leninist communism, with its top-down hierarchy, universalistic mission, and utopian belief in secular salvation, is probably better understood biblically than empirically. And I would contend that the subsequent rapid collapse of the former Soviet Union and the Soviet Empire cannot be adequately explained without reference to the subversive and transforming power of moral and spiritual forces and the resurgent role of Christianity in Eastern Europe and the Soviet Union.

The Communist collapse began, and has so far not gone significantly beyond, the European Christian world. At all of the decisive turning points, a key role was played by the resurfacing of suppressed Christian ideas and by the actions of ordinary Christians, most of whom have not yet been discovered by the historians. It all began with a simple Polish worker, the kind that the sophisticated West used to deride with Polish jokes, named Lech Walesa. And it ended in 1991 with pious old women in Moscow lecturing boys in the tanks not to fire on their cousins and brothers on the barricades. These were the old women that sociologists in the West used to deride no less than Communists in the East as the "old women in church."

The rise of the Solidarity Movement in Poland presented the Leninist Empire with a challenge to which it could not find a response. In his magisterial twelve-volume *Study of History,* Arnold Toynbee sees dominant systems breaking down only when they meet a basic challenge that they are, by their very nature, unable to deal with. Leninist systems are based on the controlled use of violence and on top-down discipline by an elite party convinced that it can crush, corrupt, or co-opt every sign of dissent. The nonviolent bottom-up Solidarity Movement in Poland with its deep religious grounding and its mass membership could not be silenced, let alone broken up. There was no head to cut off, and this Catholic movement, emboldened by the advent of a Polish pope, began the process of serially de-legitimizing Leninism and mobilizing a grassroots democratic resistance. Other such movements were aided at crucial points by Protestant pastors in Romania and East Germany, by Orthodox priests in Russia and Ukraine, and by an important Jewish element in the human rights movement within all these regions where anti-Semitism had once been rampant. Bronislaw Geremek, a key intellectual leader of Solidarity who went on to become foreign minister of Poland, had been smuggled as a child out of the Warsaw ghetto and persecuted under Communism.

A young Jewish boy was one of the three youths killed in the final showdown in Moscow during the unsuccessful coup attempt of August 1991. During the funeral procession through the streets of Moscow, as the sounds of the Hebrew Kaddish for the Jewish youth mixed with the great Church Slavonic funeral hymn "Eternal Memory" sung for the two Russian boys, they suggested reconciliation as well as a recovery of religion and of the Judeo-Christian belief in the redemptive value of innocent suffering.

When Boris Yeltsen stepped forward to address the parents of the three boys who had been killed with the simple words, "Forgive me, your President, that I was unable to defend and save your sons," he resurfaced a deep strain in Orthodoxy and, indeed, in all Christianity. "Forgive me" is what many Orthodox Russians say to whomever they are standing with, even a total stranger, before taking communion, and these are the last words of the dying heroes in two of the greatest of all Russian national operas, Musorgsky's *Boris Godunov* and Tchaikovsky's *Mazeppa.* The leader of Russia at that moment was assuming responsibility for something for which he could not be blamed and thus breaking the hold of a totalitarian system in which no one had accepted responsibility for anything. "It doesn't depend on me" was the great mantra of the Soviet system from top to bottom. Everything depended on the state; therefore, no one had any individual responsibility. The tiny democratic forces that overthrew the massed might of the Soviet system in seventy-two dramatic hours at the heart of the empire in August 1991 were not just discovering freedom in the modern, Western secular sense; they were also recovering responsibility in a traditional Eastern Christian sense.

Moral responsibility was discovered not just by the young heroes on the barricades, but also by the old women who went out to argue with the young soldiers in the tanks who never had orders to shoot. Tallyrand once said, "You can do anything with bayonets, except sit on them." The moral transformation was affecting the system itself; no one would sign a written order to shoot. I was there at the time and have written a small book about it. In a dramatic moment, the announcement came that the women should all leave, because the troops were expected to storm the Russian White House and bring to a halt this democratic resistance to a final Communist takeover. Instead of leaving, the women went to, and began talking with, the soldiers in the tanks. Lacking any word from their superiors, the soldiers in the tanks suddenly became disobedient nineteen-year-old kids who were acquiring a new chain of command. Instead of the generals it was their *babushkas* (grandmothers)—"the old women in church"—who were invoking them not to fire on their brethren.

The vacillation of the putsch leaders themselves was a result of their own assumption of moral responsibility. No one would sign or obey an order for fratricide. Almost everyone, in fact, discovered in the seventy-two hours, when the outcome was still in doubt, that they had to make individual moral decisions on their own: whether to acknowledge to one's self, to speak up to others at home or work, or to go to the barricades themselves. Among the crowd defending the headquarters of the democratic resistance, young priests ministered to people who expected to be killed in the imminent attack and, in one case, distributed two thousand Bibles to the young people on the barricades and the same number to the soldiers facing them in the tanks.

As I wandered through the streets of Moscow on the third day after the threat had passed and the outcome was clear, I heard one word being used over and over again to explain how a force with no more than 150 armed people inside that Russian White House was able to prevail against the largest uniformed army in the history of the world, five and a half million people who basically, with only a few minor exceptions, supported the coup. The word they used to explain this was *chudo,* the Russian word for miracle. It is hard to escape the feeling that some kind of a miracle was involved in this transformation of history and that the forces that were at work are not yet in the history books.

For some Orthodox believers, the explanation lay not in the new social sciences, but in the Russian Orthodox Church calendar itself. The crisis had begun on the Feast of the Transfiguration, when the coup was launched and the first resistance formed. It had ended on the Feast of the Assumption, when a liturgy in the Kremlin Cathedral of the Assumption sanctified the opening of the first post-Communist parliament in Russia. In the interim, their country had been transformed, if not transfigured, and their people had been protected from bloodshed by what had traditionally been the ultimate security policy in the Christian East: appeals for intercession to the Virgin Mary or, as she is called in the Eastern churches, the Mother of God. In a prayer broadcast on the loudspeakers, the patriarch had in fact publicly invoked her on behalf of the resistance at the exact time in the second night when an attack had been most expected. Those two feasts in the Christian East—the Feast of the Transfiguration, in memory of Christ's first appearance to his disciples in his transfigured state on Mount Tabor, and the Feast of the Assumption, the Virgin's final entry as the Mother of God into heaven—are among the least understood in Western, and particularly Protestant, Christianity. In his novel, *Dr. Zhivago*, Pasternak sees the revolution as a kind of re-enactment of the Passion of Holy Week. This kind of liturgical and biblical frame was seen as an explanation of the history unfolding today by those who were rediscovering their Christian heritage.

In the most violent century in human history, the twentieth century, the Cold War ended suddenly and peacefully in a way that seemed to hold out promise for the new century and the new millennium. Like the civil rights movement in America and the human rights movement globally, the power that transformed the Soviet Communist Empire was a nonviolent movement, rooted in religion rising from below rather than in secular ideologies imposed from above—in a movement seeking evolutionary rather than revolutionary change, practical modifications rather than utopian dreams.

The Future of Christianity

Russia's hopes for the future, about which I am personally optimistic, depend largely on whether or not the Russian people will be able to construct a new political and economic system that will give scope to freedom but at the same time recover their own moral and religious traditions that will alone be able to link freedom with its Siamese twin of responsibility. Post-Soviet Russia has given to Christianity not only a host of new converts, but a chance to learn about a host of inspiring martyrs that neither we nor they have fully recognized.

The magnificent new second edition of the *World Christian Encyclopedia* estimates that 64 percent of all the authenticated 70 million martyrs in Christian history occurred in the twentieth century—almost all of them in either Communist or third-world dictatorial regimes. Christianity has always grown in times of martyrdom and is growing not only in former Communist countries, but even more rapidly in the developing countries of the Third World. The net defections from Christianity in Europe and North America, on the other hand, are shown to be now running at nearly two million a year. The number of Christians in the world's 172 least-developed nations grew in the twentieth century from 83 million to 1 billion 120 million, increasing 38-fold in Africa alone. While Christianity is growing almost everywhere else except in the advanced Western world, so too are other religions whose civilizations are being propelled into modernity—not just by economic globalization, but also by the audio-visual and digital communication revolution that comes out of America, but so far treats the outside world as customers to be cultivated rather than cultures to be understood.

If you cannot learn to listen to other people when they are whispering their prayers, you may have to meet them later on the battlefield when they are howling their war cries. At the very time when peaceful evolutionary progress seemed assured, we have been confronted with a hideous new face of violence that spreads terror through the new audio-visual media the way revolution was spread through the new medium of telegraphy in the mid-nineteenth century. When telegraphy first came to Russia as it began modernizing under its most reform-minded tsar, Alexander II, Russia produced in the late 1870s the first human association to adopt the word "terrorism" as a badge of honor and pride. Central to these original terrorists were programs of carefully planned political assassination, which eventually succeeded in killing Alexander himself in 1881. They believed that terror and intimidation would be greatly magnified by the expanded press coverage, not just of their violence, but also of the selfless dedication of the perpetrators. Today a new generation of terrorists is using the second great transborder communication revolution, the audio-visual and digital revolutions of our time, in a similar way. This new horror must be combatted for the evil that it is and for the threat it poses not only to life and limb, but to the nonviolent evolutionary development and spiritual renewal that are in many ways the most constructive forces of our time.

Conclusion

Now let me, as I move toward conclusion, return for a moment to our own post–Cold War America. I believe that we will never understand, let alone respect, the deep and the positive part of the faith of others unless we are able to recover the deep and positive part of our own faith. A nation that has lost the living links with its own heritage of worship and service and prayer will hardly be able to understand, let alone properly respect, the faith traditions of others. There is particular need to understand three worlds of more than a billion people, with deep cultures and religions of their own, that are now emerging into full participation in world history: the Islamic world from Indonesia to Morocco, the Hindu sub-continent of South Asia, and the Confucian-based world of China and East Asia.

It is sometimes said that all roads up Mount Fujiyama meet at the top, but I believe we meet others better by digging into the roots, for it is by sharing memory and stories that we find our commonalities. American pluralism has always assumed a plurality of authentic convictions, rather than the monism of indifference that we so often meet today. Cardinal George of Chicago suggested in a marvelous speech at a bicentennial colloquium we had at the Library of Congress last year that Christians in America today should ask others: What are the gifts you have to bring to the table? He suggested that Christians should be gently subversive of our own pagan culture, yet remain open to those gifts that others will bring—and in the process deepen and recover our own faith.

Some of the deepest students of our culture have suggested that poetry can help us cope with the future better than the prose of historians or the predictions of social scientists. So I am going to close with poetry from three different cultures.

First, from Russia comes a poem that came back to me when reading about a group of Christian martyrs in a Soviet death camp. A group of women who wanted to celebrate an Easter service there were told that they could do so only if they conducted it standing in a slowly freezing lake.

They did so singing out "Christ is risen," the Easter greeting of Orthodoxy, before freezing to death.

Another group of women came on the first Easter and found nobody in the tomb. As the Gospel of Luke tells it, they "were afraid and bowed down their faces to the earth." Then came a voice that said, "Why do you seek the living among the dead? He is not here, he is risen." The word for living in the liturgical Slavonic version of that text is *zhivago*, the title of the great testament to Christian hope written by Boris Pasternak just as the last great systematic campaign to stamp out religion was being launched in the USSR in the late 1950s. The novel ends with a poetic view of history that sees future relevance in the deep interior Christianity of the Russian past:

> You see, the passing of years is like a parable
> Which can, at any time, catch fire along the way.
> In the name of its terrible majesty
> I go down, a voluntary victim, to my grave.
> I go into my grave, and on the third day rise
> And like little boats spread across a river
> Towards me to judgment, like a caravan of barges
> The centuries flow forward out of darkness.

A second poem, written by a great American poet of the last century, T. S. Eliot, reflects on the trauma of his experience as he witnessed the incendiary bombs engulfing London with flames in 1940. Many people have recently compared the terrible tragedy in New York, those sudden flames that seemed to be engulfing and threatening civilization itself, with that time when Britain stood alone. Eliot seems to have seen the symbolic tongues of fire with which the Holy Spirit descended on the first apostles as somehow being the ultimate weapon against the fires with which Hitler was reigning evil on England. And so at the end of the last of his *Four Quartets*, Eliot writes:

> The dove descending breaks the air
> with flame of incandescent terror
> of which the tongues declare
> the one discharged from sin and error
> the only hope or else despair
> lies in the choice of pyre or pyre.

To be redeemed from fire by fire
Who then devised the torment love?
Love is the unfamiliar name behind the hands
that wove the intolerable shirt of flame
which human power cannot remove.
We only live only suspire
consumed by either fire or fire.
History is a pattern of timeless moments
so while the light fails on a winter's afternoon in a secluded chapel.
History is now in England with a drawing of this love
And the voice of this calling.
We shall not cease from exploration
and the end of all of our exploring
will be to arrive where we started.
And know the place for the first time.
A condition of complete simplicity
costing not less than everything
and all shall be well and all manner of things shall be well.
When the tongues of flame are enfolded
into the crowned knot of fire
and the fire and the rose are one.

An unknown European priest writing for a nonexistent Asian audience in an already dead language wrote the third poem I have chosen. Somehow these lines suggest to me that, whether or not we in the West will be able better to understand other parts of the world or even our own past, we will be ennobled by the continuing effort.

When the Jesuit order finally left China after the most deeply scholarly and most nearly successful effort in history to build a cultural bridge between the Christian West and the most ancient of Eastern cultures, they left behind as their last legacy a haunting epitaph:

> *Abi, viator*
> *Congratulare mortuis*
> *Condole vives*
> *Ora pro omnibus*
> *Mirare e tace.*

Move on, voyager
Congratulate the dead
Console the living
Pray for everyone
Wonder and be silent.

Chapter Two

How the Religious Past Frames America's Future

Mark A. Noll

Since social contexts always make a great difference for any prophetic endeavor, it is perhaps actually fitting to think about major changes in American religion during the twentieth century, particularly for how such changes might affect prospects for a responsible religious life in the future. And so I would like first to examine five developments of the past century that would have been extremely difficult for even the most prescient observer in 1900 to predict. This historical exercise will take up the majority of our time, but at the end I do want to reflect briefly on how these unexpected twentieth-century developments shape the world in which we now live.

The five surprising developments that I would like to highlight are

1. a remarkable resurrection of the Holy Spirit
2. an explosive expansion of religious diversity
3. a dramatic displacement of mainline to margins and margins to mainline
4. an unexpected engagement between Protestants and Roman Catholics
5. a surprising surge of ethnic Christianity

MARK A. NOLL, McManis Professor of Christian Thought at Wheaton College, includes among his books the following: *Religion and American Politics, The Old Religion in a New World: A History of North American Christianity, The Scandal of the Evangelical Mind,* and *The Search for Christian America.*

Remarkable Resurrection of the Holy Spirit

In 1900, there were no, or virtually no, Pentecostal Christians on the face of the planet. Today Pentecostalism is—in many different manifestations—the fastest growing, most diverse form of Christianity in the whole world.[1] The cradle of this new Christian movement was an abandoned Methodist church at 312 Azusa Street in the industrial section of Los Angeles where in 1906 William J. Seymour (1870–1922), a mild-mannered Black holiness preacher, founded the Apostolic Faith Gospel Mission. Soon Seymour's emphasis on the work of the Holy Spirit, which he had learned from Charles Fox Parham, a teacher himself shaped by Methodist and holiness traditions, was a local sensation. The revival that began on Azusa Street in 1906 was marked by fervent prayer, speaking in tongues, earnest new hymns, and healing of the sick. One of its most prominent features was the full participation of women in public activities. In an America that still took racial barriers for granted, Azusa Street was also remarkable, at least initially, for the striking way that Blacks and Hispanics joined Whites in the nightly meetings. Soon the Azusa Street chapel became a mecca for thousands of visitors from around the world, who often went back to their homelands proclaiming the need for a special postconversion baptism of the Holy Spirit. From a number of new alliances, networks of periodicals, and circuits of preachers and faith-healers, the Assemblies of God, established in 1914, emerged as the most important Pentecostal denomination among Caucasians.[2] Less than a century later, there are now about 12,000 Assemblies of God congregations in the United States ministering to nearly two and one-half million adherents, and indigenous churches begun by Assemblies of God missionaries outside the United States have multiplied the outreach of this one denomination many times over.

For African-Americans, Pentecostalism opened a highway to energetic church formation and dynamic personal spirituality. Under the leadership of Charles H. Mason, the Church of God in Christ has become one of the largest Protestant denominations of any type in the United States as well as an active promoter of Pentecostal forms of the faith overseas.

Later observers have noted that Pentecostalism spread most rapidly among self-disciplined, often mobile folk of the middle and lower-middle classes. But an ardent desire for the unmediated experience of the Holy Spirit was a still more common characteristic. It is difficult to overemphasize the general impact of Pentecostal influence. Practices of Christian worship at the end of the century attest most obviously to the scope of that influence.

Pentecostal worship has always been exuberant, spontaneous, and subjective. In the early decades of the movement a great quantity of new hymns were written to express the heightened emotions resulting from direct contact with the Spirit. But Pentecostal patterns of worship and religious practice only began to have a broader impact on the wider religious world when a pair of developments occurred after World War II. First was the rise in public meetings for healing led by evangelists like William Branham (1909–1965) and Oral Roberts (b. 1918). The second, even more important development was the beginning of the charismatic movement in the late 1950s. This movement promoted some of the emphases of classical Pentecostalism. But it promoted them in typical American fashion by presenting a kind of spiritual smorgasbord to sample as individuals chose. Charismatic emphases included a stress on personal conversion, physical healing, speaking in tongues, participation in small group fellowships, and freshly written songs—but always as a range of open possibilities rather than formal requirements. Charismatic (in the other sense of the term) leaders have also played a major role in the charismatic (in the religious sense of the term) movement.

Charismatic renewal has taken many forms. It provided a bridge of common associations, songs, and attitudes between Pentecostals and non-Pentecostals. The charismatic movement also entered the Catholic Church where it continues to exert a persistent influence. More often it took shape in parachurch organizations like the Full Gospel Business Men's Fellowship, International. And it has also influenced recent associations of churches that draw on the emphases of the movement. These have included the Calvary Chapels under the leadership of Chuck Smith, whose mixture of informality, soft rock music, biblical exposition, and the standard charismatic options has led to a network of more than 600 Calvary Chapels around the world. A similar story can be told about the Association of Vineyard Churches. Under the leadership of founder John Wimber, this California-based evangelical movement has stressed divine healing and promoted nontraditional forms of worship. It has grown to over 300 congregations with more than 100,000 members and with congregations in many countries outside of the United States. Pentecostal and charismatic traditions are also essential for understanding the widely reported revivals that continue at the Airport Vineyard Fellowship in Toronto and the Brownsville Assembly of God church in Pensacola, Florida.

Effects of charismatic influence include greater concern for specific acts of the Holy Spirit, but even more a general turn toward subjective spirituality, even in churches where specific Pentecostal teachings are unknown. The great changes in church music that began to take place in the 1960s were almost all related to the charismatic movement. Many congregations and fellowships began to sing newly written choruses and Scripture texts set to fresh melodies. By the 1980s church musicians were exploiting a full range of pop, folk, and even rock styles as settings for this new wave of song. The increasingly common practice of singing with a combo made up of guitar, drums, and synthesizer has begun to push aside the organ as the instrument of choice in many Protestant and some Catholic churches. Songs projected by an overhead onto a screen have supplemented or replaced the hymn book in many places. The same set of religious forces has provided the foundation for a multimillion-dollar industry of contemporary Christian music.

Critics of Pentecostalism, the charismatic movement, and other Protestant adaptations to modern sensibilities are not shy about expressing their disapproval.[3] They charge that charismatic worship focuses on the self and not on God. They see the megachurches as catering to the transitory felt-needs of a pleasure-driven population. They hold that modern innovations obscure the realities of human sinfulness and the holiness of God and so make it impossible to grasp the true character of divine grace. Such debates reprise many earlier arguments in American religious history, as between the Methodists and their opponents at the start of the nineteenth century. These debates are important because they address the twin, but sometimes competing, strengths of American Christianity. These strengths are connection to the historic Christian faith and a drive to gain adherents for that faith within the world's most liberal and most democratic culture.

By way of summary, it is possible to say that in the first two-thirds of the twentieth century forms of Baptist and mainline spirituality competed for dominance in the United States, but toward the end of the century both seem to be giving way to the various emphases of charismatic faith and practice.

Explosive Expansion of Religious Diversity

The flourishing of charismatic and Pentecostal religion has been a major factor in a second development of the last century, which was an explosive expansion of religious diversity. Compared to the rest of the world in 1900, the United States was unusually pluralistic in its range of religious expression. Compared to the year 2000, however, the diversity present at the beginning of the century was only a pale shadow of what it has become. Even when limiting consideration only to Christian groups, the United States now enjoys an unprecedented, staggering degree of organizational Christian pluraformity.

Even to grasp the outlines of that diversity is a formidable task. Within the United States are to be found fourteen separate Eastern Orthodox churches that register their existence with national clearing-houses, and there are probably several more which do not.[4] Among Protestants, institutional creativity is almost beyond accounting. In the *Encyclopedia of American Religions* (5th edition, 1996), J. Gordon Melton lists nineteen separate Presbyterian denominations, thirty-two Lutheran, thirty-six Methodist, thirty-seven Episcopal or Anglican, sixty Baptist, and 241 Pentecostal. Even if a few of these denominations are little more than single congregations, and even though Melton included Canadian denominations in lists, the number of such groupings is still staggering.

For Catholics, the hierarchical structures linking the faithful to Rome nonetheless cannot mask the profusion of theological, racial, educational, ideological, social, linguistic, and cultural sub-groups within its single church. Many commentators have made the point that, because of internal differences over the course of Catholicism since the Second Vatican Council and because of fissures remaining from an earlier ethnic history, the Catholic church now has almost as many sub-divisions, interest groups, lobbies, and shades of opinions as can be found in the wide world of Protestantism. American Catholics remain united by their common Roman identification, but some of them think Pope John Paul II has been a disaster for the church while others think he has been the greatest pope in modern times; many blithely disregard the church's dogma prohibiting artificial birth control while others support it; some regard Vatican II as a charter for liberalization while others think it enlivened the traditions of the church and so on.

Moreover, diversity among Protestant denominations and within the

Catholic Church only begins to tell the story of America's Christian pluralism. Within the borders of the United States exists also a bewildering
array of newer, sectarian movements. Some of these, like the Church of
Jesus Christ of Latter-day Saints (Mormons), have increasingly taken on
church-like status and functions. Others like the Jehovah's Witnesses remain closer to their original sectarian character, but with nearly one million members it is an important factor in American religion. Still other
once-sectarian groups, like the Seventh-day Adventists or the Worldwide
Church of God have in recent decades come to emphasize more their commonality with historic Protestantism and less the distinctives of their
founding.[5]

But even a roster of denominations and denomination-like groups still
only begins to chart the full measure of diversity. It is necessary also to take
account of what the British sociologist David Martin has called "the
buzzing complex of voluntary organizations" found in the United States to
complete the picture.[6] Among Protestants, there have always existed more
associations, groups, and societies outside the churches than as churches.
The effects of World War II in putting millions of people into new places,
new occupations, and new associations, combined with the postwar economic boom, only multiplied the quantity of such groups. Their range—
from the Southern Christian Leadership Conference to the Christian
Coalition, from the Concerned Women of America and Women Aglow
through Bread for the World and Clergy and Laity Concerned to Promise
Keepers and on and on—is nearly overwhelming.

The extent of American Christian diversity means that it is almost impossible to predict the theological, social, or political consequence of nominal religious adherence. An outstanding book by historian Charles Marsh
on the dramatic civil rights confrontations of 1964 in the state of Mississippi provides a clear illustration of that reality. Marsh found that all of the
major participants were Protestants, and yet extraordinarily different kinds
of Protestants. They included Fannie Lou Hamer, an African-American
leader of the Mississippi Freedom Democratic Party, who once was sustained by thoughts of Jesus as she was being savagely beaten in the
Winona, Mississippi, city jail. But they also included Sam Bowers, Imperial Wizard of the White Knights of the Ku Klux Klan, who saw himself defending the sovereignty of God and the resurrection of Jesus Christ in his
conspiracy to murder three civil rights workers. The other principals were
not as extreme, but they too illustrated the very diverse paths that Christ-

ian allegiance took in this one situation and that it regularly takes in other American settings.[7]

Mainline to Margins and Margins to Mainline

Amidst the bloomin', buzzin' confusion of American religious diversity, however, at least one important generalization rises to the surface; it is a dramatic displacement of mainline to margins and margins to mainline. Into the 1930s, American religion seemed to maintain its traditional picture, which might be described as a mainline traditional Protestant Snow White surrounded by a multitude of scurrying little dwarves. That picture began to change visibly with the crises of mainline Protestants during the era of the Depression. The public turmoils of the 1960s accelerated the decline of the old mainline Protestants. At the end of the century it is increasingly obvious that these older, proprietary bodies that had done so much to shape American life in the nineteenth century have struggled to adjust.[8] For some, the difficulty seemed to be a top-heavy bureaucracy trying to run churches like corporations. For others, controversy over beliefs seemed to impede vigorous action. The colleges and seminaries of these older, mostly northern bodies were the centers of a generally liberal theology. That theology stressed human capacities more than traditional views of God's loving power. It tended to accent what humans could do for themselves in this life instead of how religion prepared people for heaven. Sometimes it waffled in providing moral guidelines for church members. To the extent that such beliefs prevailed in the older denominations, or were even thought to prevail, the churches lost credibility with some of their constituents and failed to recruit new members. By contrast, denominations that stressed traditional beliefs about the supernatural power of God and the reliability of the Bible, or that featured the newer Pentecostal emphases on the immediate action of the Holy Spirit, continued to expand.

Specific numbers provide some help in charting these changes. The steady growth of the Catholic Church has made it overwhelmingly the largest Christian denomination in the country. Where the national population grew 108 percent between 1940 and 2000, Catholic adherents grew 191 percent. With something over sixty-two million adherents in 2000, the Catholic Church in the United States is larger than the total population of either the United Kingdom or France.

The greatest contrast to Catholic growth is mainline Protestant losses. From 1960 to 2000, and taking account of the denominational mergers of intervening years, the Presbyterian Church (USA) has suffered a net decline of about 550,000; the Episcopal Church a decline of 900,000; the United Church of Christ (which incorporates most of the Congregationalists) a decline of over 800,000; the Disciples of Christ a decline of over 900,000; and the United Methodist Church a decline of over two million members. It must be kept in mind that these are large enough denominations so that, for example, the Methodists still enjoy over eight million members, and the others enjoy the adherence of from one to three million each. But the declines are still substantial.

The older ethnic churches—Lutherans, Reformed, Mennonites, ethnic Baptists—have fared somewhat better, with some growing substantially after World War II. But the growth rate for such denominations has lagged considerably behind the growth rate of national population at least since 1960.

The Protestant bodies whose rates of growth in recent decades have exceeded general population increases, sometimes far exceeded, are nearly all characterized by labels like Bible-believing, born again, conservative, evangelical, fundamentalist, holiness, Pentecostal, or restorationist.[9] They include the Assemblies of God, the Christian and Missionary Alliance, the Church of God in Christ, the Seventh-day Adventists, the Church of the Nazarene, the Salvation Army, the Baptist Bible Fellowship International, the Churches of Christ, the Church of the Nazarene, and several more of this sort. To provide comparisons with the older mainline churches, between 1960 and 2000, the Assemblies of God grew by two million members; the Black Pentecostal Church of God in Christ by at least that many millions; the Church of God (Cleveland, Tennessee) by about 600,000; the Seventh-day Adventists by over 500,000, and the Church of the Nazarene by over 300,000. During that same period the Church of Jesus Christ of Latter-day Saints (Mormons) added a net of three and a half million members.

The largest Protestant denomination since at least the middle of the century has been the Southern Baptist Convention. Despite the bruising internal struggle it experienced in the 1970s and 1980s, the Convention has continued on a similar path of expansion. It is indicative of more general trends among Protestants that the conservatives won the Southern Baptists' internal struggle, and that the Southern Baptist Convention grew from 1960 to 2000 by six million members and at a pace considerably higher than the rate of national population growth.

Increasingly sophisticated procedures in survey research have revealed that about one in four Americans (or 25 percent) is now affiliated with a church from this network of conservative Protestant churches (that is, fundamentalist, evangelical, holiness, or Pentecostal). Not quite one in six (around 15 percent) are affiliated with the older denominations that used to be called the Protestant mainline.[10]

These denominational shifts seem to indicate that churches providing relatively clear boundaries for belief and practice, relatively sharp affirmation of the supernatural, and relatively more demands on their members have done better in modern America than those which have not.[11]

Protestant-Catholic Engagement

The shifting landscape of denominational affiliation draws attention to what might be considered a mega-shift in the unexpected engagement between Protestants and Roman Catholics. In late 1983, the conservative Anglican theologian, J. I. Packer, began a book review with a revealing bit of autobiography. Packer had been nurtured in the literature of the English Puritans; his published writings had gained him renown in Britain, Canada, and the United States as one of the most articulate modern advocates of thoughtful Reformed Anglicanism.[12] Packer's remarks about the book, which was called *The Born-Again Catholic*, spoke of a momentous alteration in a long-standing religious quarrel:

> If when I was a student you had told me that before old age struck I should be reviewing a popular Roman Catholic book on the new birth which used Campus Crusade material, carried an official *nihil obstat* and *imprimatur*, and was already in its fourth printing in three years, I doubt whether I would have believed you. But that is what I am doing now. Again, if at that time you had predicted that one day an Anglican bishop would tell me how the last Roman Catholic priest to whom he talked quizzed him hard as to whether Anglicans really preached the new birth as they should, I would probably have laughed in your face. But this month it happened. Things are not as they were![13]

Packer's remarks point to a seismic change in religious history. Into the

1960s, the antagonism between Catholics and Protestants that began over three centuries earlier seemed permanent. One of the very few fixed planets in the religious sky of Western civilization seemed to be the finality of Catholic-Protestant antagonism.

The Protestant brief against Catholicism was expressed in a Niagara of books, pamphlets, and sermons so voluminous that no one human could possibly take the measure of it all. But the main points of that brief can be summarized quite easily. Catholics, in Protestant view,

- taught that people earned their salvation by doing good deeds
- prevented common people from reading the Bible and from taking their guidance for life from the Scriptures
- manufactured extra-biblical saints, festivals, and rites that substituted human imagination for biblical patterns of worship
- took away glory from Christ by making Mary a co-author of salvation
- wantonly corrupted Scripture by forcing new doctrines onto the people merely at the whim of popes and councils whose supposed authority was no more than the imperialistic expression of their own selfish ambition
- promoted a corrupting hierarchy that stripped the faithful of their proper status as priests before God

In their turn, Catholics gave as good as they got. Wherever Catholic communities were placed in physical or intellectual connection with Protestants, a literature sprouted that reversed the charges. Rather than rescuing Christianity from corruption, Protestantism was hastening it toward decay. In Catholic view, Protestants

- offered a "salvation" by faith that denied the need for holiness before God
- abandoned the Bible to the interpretation of every Tom, Dick, and Mary (no matter how bizarre those interpretations might be) and so effectively stripped the Bible of normative, authoritative meaning
- denied the ability of the Holy Spirit to work through ongoing teaching officers in the church as the Spirit had early worked in bringing the church into existence

- scandalously neglected God's gracious help provided to humanity in the person of the Blessed Virgin Mary and the exemplary saints
- rejected the apostolic authority of bishops, councils, and popes and so abetted the rising Western tide of rationalism, secularism, and moral anarchy
- forsook genuine ecclesiastical leadership in favor of a political free-for-all where authority was reduced to merely the power of manipulation

These polemics, which have echoed around the world since the mid-sixteenth century, were a fixture in the United States until very recently indeed.

In the United States, moreover, Protestants were leaders in arguing that Catholicism was not only a religious threat, but also that it subverted the free political institutions of the United States. Into the late 1950s almost no one could have predicted that change was in the air.

That was then. Only short decades later, the situation has become very different. The most visible public signal of a shift in the United States was the election of a Catholic as president in 1960. John F. Kennedy's victory was itself a milestone for overcoming Protestant bias and fulfilling earlier Catholic efforts at public service. The circumstances of the 1960 campaign added even greater symbolic importance to Kennedy's election. His famous campaign speech before Protestant ministers in Houston seemed to convince them, and many others, that a Catholic president would not imperil national integrity. Kennedy's scrupulous record on church-state matters, particularly his opposition to government aid for parochial schools, silenced many critics who feared that Catholics did not have proper national priorities. On this issue Billy Graham spoke for others by bestowing the indelicate praise that Kennedy had turned out to be a Baptist president.[14] Moreover, the apotheosis which occurred after Kennedy's assassination left him, a Roman Catholic, one of the most popular American presidents among the public at large. The religious issue in American politics, though not yet dead, had suffered a crushing blow. Even Kennedy's misdeeds have helped defuse inter-religious antagonisms, for his womanizing and power-grabbing were "ecumenical" in resembling the misdeeds of politicians who happened to be Protestant.

The Kennedy phenomenon, however, was less significant for long-term improvement in Protestant-Catholic relations than more strictly religious events which, after having been set in motion in Rome, led to great changes in America. Even before Pope John XXIII convened the Second Vatican Council in 1962, he had established a Secretariat for Promoting Christian Unity in the Vatican. In the wake of the Council's Decree on Ecumenism, which commends this work to the bishops everywhere in the world for their diligent and prudent guidance, the Conference of American Bishops in November 1964 set up its own Ecumenical Commission. This agency sponsored subcommissions which very soon were deep in discussion with the Orthodox Church in the United States and with several of the major Protestant traditions.[15] Of these meetings, that between Lutherans and Catholics has produced the richest fruit, with a series of agreements on the Nicene Creed, baptism, the Eucharist and, most importantly, justification by faith.[16] Catholic entrance into ecumenical activity has continued on a broad level.

In light of how important the civic sphere has always been for Catholic-evangelical relations, it is not surprising that an alteration in political perception contributed greatly to the changes of recent decades. Several developments since the 1960s have conspired to extinguish (or at least greatly diminish) the Protestant fear of Catholicism as a civil threat. American Catholics were among the leaders at the Second Vatican Council in securing strong statements on behalf of civil liberty. In the international arena, even more damage was done to Protestant notions of Catholic tyranny by the contribution of the Catholic Church to the Solidarity movement in Poland, the public leadership of Pope John Paul II in combating communism in Europe, and the pope's temperate statements on explosive political situations in Latin America, Africa, and Asia.[17] These political actions did not address doctrinal issues directly, but they did strip away much of the civil anxiety with which American Protestants had always looked upon Roman Catholics.

The practicalities of local political action have also done much to open doorways. Over the last several decades, contemporary political affairs have become so passionately tangled that Christian faiths and public stances on moral issues now collide in nearly every conceivable combination. The crucible effect wrought by this situation explains why many Catholic-Protestant barriers have fallen: committed toilers in the public vineyard have glanced up in surprise to find previously despised Catholics or Protestants laboring right alongside.

On specific theological issues, the ecumenical dialogues promoted by the Second Vatican Council have gone a considerable distance toward clarifying the difference between mistaken religious stereotypes and genuine theological disagreement. All of the Catholic dialogues with different Protestant groups have highlighted areas of continuing disagreement. But those same dialogues have also cast some historic standoffs into a startlingly new light. While sectarian, evangelical, fundamentalist, and Pentecostal Protestants have usually not kept abreast of the various Catholic-Protestant dialogues, their contents make fascinating reading for anyone with even a little knowledge of the historic standoff between Catholics and Protestants.

The significance of these American discussions was heightened many times over when on October 31, 1999—Reformation Sunday—representatives of the Vatican and the Lutheran World Federation signed a document affirming at that much broader level a mostly common understanding of justification by faith. Its basic affirmation signaled unprecedented progress in addressing the disputes of the Reformation: "Together we confess: By grace alone, in faith in Christ's saving work and not because of any merit on our part, we are accepted by God and receive the Holy Spirit, who renews our hearts while equipping and calling us to do good works."[18]

By no means is it the case that Protestant-Catholic differences have vanished. It is the case, however, that relations between these once stony antagonists have softened over the last 40 years in ways that observers as late as 1950 could not possibly have imagined.

Surprising Surge of Ethnic Christianity

A last major change of the century is the surprising surge of ethnic Christianity. Throughout the latter decades of the twentieth century, the new "ethnic churches" have become an ever larger part of the American religious story. Where identifiable religious forms inherited from Britain and Northern Europe have faded into more general American patterns, African-Americans have retained distinctive religious practices. In addition, Asian-Americans and Hispanics have recently become increasingly important in the overall Christian picture. Within the mix of Protestant churches, an increasingly large share is made up by adherents of which might be called the new ethnic churches. Of the nation's Protestants, about one-sixth are now African-Americans, and the numbers of both Asian-

American and Hispanic Protestants reach into the millions, even as Hispanic-Americans make up an ever-increasing proportion of the Catholic Church.

Hispanics still remain largely identified with the Catholic Church but also reflect the profound changes of recent years. The American Catholic hierarchy concentrates much energy on reaching and encouraging the Catholic Hispanic population, in part because of long-existing practices of nominal participation and in part because of recent inroads by Protestants, especially Pentecostals. Predictions vary, but all observers see Hispanics becoming an ever larger, perhaps even a majority, presence in the American church in a very few years.

The activities and goals of Hispanic Catholics in the United States naturally reflect broader developments in Latin America. The assemblies of Latin American bishops at Medellín, Colombia, in 1968 and in Puebla, Mexico, in 1979, focused Catholic energies on the crying needs of Latin America's poor. Neither Pope Paul VI nor Pope John Paul II favored Marxist solutions to the burgeoning urban poverty of Latin America, but both encouraged the church to act aggressively in bringing the gospel as well as material assistance to those in need. Such themes have resonated as well in areas of the United States with strong Hispanic populations. In the manner of earlier generations of Catholic immigrants, Hispanic Catholics are also finding ways of incorporating their ancestral traditions of devotion and festival in an American setting.[19]

Protestantism among American Hispanics has been given a tremendous boost by the Pentecostal movement. Hispanics took part in the earliest Pentecostal moments of Asuza Street and as early as 1916, Puerto Ricans who had received the gift of tongues returned to their native land to establish a Pentecostal presence there. In the last quarter of the century, Pentecostal Hispanic churches have been among the fastest growing churches in North America. Unlike the Presbyterians and Methodists, who hesitated to establish Spanish-speaking districts, Pentecostal denominations like the Assemblies of God have regularly followed this practice, with the result that Hispanic sections of Pentecostal denominations flourish in California, Texas, the Southwest, and some northern urban centers.

The recent immigration of Asians is also working its effects on the American churches. Identification with Christianity is linked with immigration to the United States, with the result that almost all Asian-American populations (Korean, Chinese, Japanese, Vietnamese, Thai, and others) have a higher percentage of Christian allegiance than populations in the Asian lands. Korean-Americans have been especially active in forming churches on the West Coast and in several major cities of the North, although Koreans with all other Asian-American Christian groups face the very difficult problem of keeping their American-born young people satisfied with combined Asian and American religious practice. While not overlooking the reality of such difficulties, it is still the case that a heightened visibility of ethnic Christian churches has been one of the most dramatic developments of the past century.

Religion, Scholarship, and the American Future

These major surprises in twentieth-century American religious history do not by themselves yield easy predictions about the future. Large-scale developments in culture and society also exert great force. Life expectancy, for example, has greatly increased over the course of the century, especially for female Americans; a world where longevity into the 70s, 80s, and even 90s is much, much more common than 100 years ago is a different world for religion as for everything else. It is the same for general family structure, where divorce has become much more common and the presence of large extended families much less common. Similarly, a world in which there was no radio, television, or Internet is obviously a much different world from one in which these electronic media have become ubiquitous. In addition, it is difficult to exaggerate how significant it was in 1900 that there existed in the United States seventeen clergymen for every one college professor, whereas today the professors outnumber the clergy by about two to one.[20] All of these serious changes *outside* the churches strictly considered obviously have tremendous implications on life *within* the churches.

Any thoughts about the future of religion in the United States must be tentative, in light of how many unexpected developments occurred over the last century and when considering how much influence is always exerted on religious thought and practice by broad social and cultural changes. Still, it is worth making an effort to look ahead, and so I will venture a few words on three subjects: American Christianity and the intellectual life, American Christianity and politics, and American Christianity and the rest of the Christian world.

The changing American religious landscape seems to me surprisingly propitious for the intellectual life. As some of you may realize, I am *not* a particular fan of what America's sectarian, evangelical, fundamentalist, or Pentecostal Protestants have produced intellectually or artistically over the course of the twentieth century. I am, however, convinced that a prerequisite for serious religious thought is serious religion. From studies of the modern university by George Marsden, Philip Gleason, James Burtchaell, and others, it is clear that active Christian life is certainly a necessary condition, even if it is not by itself sufficient condition for active Christian thinking. The decline of mainline Protestant higher education as well as the current confusion in Catholic higher education has come about partly as a result of problems with *thinking*. Much more, they have resulted from a loss of *spiritual* direction.

The encouraging thing for the Christian intellectual future from recent American history is the sheer presence of active Christian communities. At the start of the twenty-first century, the centers of meaningful religious life among Christians are overwhelmingly Pentecostal, charismatic, Baptist, ethnic, evangelical, fundamentalist, and sectarian Protestant in some combination, or some variety of committed Catholicism. If these groups have not yet produced a whole lot of stellar intellectual leadership, they nonetheless include great numbers of active and earnest Christians. The intellectual work produced to date by these cohorts has been minimal. In literary art, the situation is worse. Mainline Protestants are spared the oceans of literary *dreck* that infest the worlds of conservative Protestants only because mainline Protestantism produces so little literary work of any sort that can be traced to the inner dynamics of religious faith. The encouraging thing about the American religious landscape is not that the active, energetic, growing movements of sectarian and conservative Protestants have produced great quantities of significant intellectual or literary work; it is rather that they exist. And it is easier to move from bad writing to good writing than it is to move from weak religion to strong religion.

Since I am a historian, I dare not end an assessment of intellectual life on a positive note. The American religious situation at the start of a new century does, it seems to me, show definite signs of hope with respect to the life of the mind. But it also offers real occasion for worry. One worry is that Christian intellectuals will not be able to discriminate between helpful and harmful currents in the academy at large. Christian intellectuals can be strengthened, sharpened, and fruitfully challenged by participation in broader intellectual life, but not if they fall prey to the enervating skepticism, the trendy relativism, and the self-defeating identity politics of that arena. The tremendous diversity that now characterizes American Christianity means that there are many active communities of religious vitality. It also means that very few of these communities of religious vitality have anything like the intellectual weight required for standing firm and with discrimination in the modern academy. The onus, therefore, falls on individual Christian scholars and elective small groups of such scholars to promote the balance that the churches, denominations, and parachurch agencies by and large do not provide.

A related issue concerns the nature of the religion that has increasingly come to the fore in American churches. The vitality of expressive, affectional, self-affirming, therapeutic, entertaining, and mobile religion has, it seems to me, much to commend it. Whether this kind of what might be called yogurt religion can, however, provide the fiber, the protein, for serious artistic or intellectual endeavor remains to be seen. To be filled with the Spirit is a good thing. To speak with the tongues of men and of angels may also be a good thing. But unless the Spirit-filled also master the languages *of* this world, they will, in the end, have very little to say *in* this world.

The Christian Political Future

Let me attempt now a few words on the Christian political future. I remember well attending a small meeting right at the end of 1996 or early in 1997 when Bill Clinton's re-election to a second term as president was the subject. One of the people present had recently received two urgent letters from the heads of Christian agencies. When these letters were passed around, it was clear how stark were the alternatives confronting America's Christian believers with respect to issues of political activity. One of the letters was a battle cry—the Enemy, in the person of President Clinton, had landed, and it was now time to mobilize all possible energy, money, time, talent, legal assistance, and radio time to fight this menace to the death. The other letter was very different. It urged breaking off from further political strife in order to recapture the purity of private Christian life and the imperatives of world evangelization. My opinion remains now what it was when I first read these two letters: politics *was* important, but not in the all-consuming, all-or-nothing mode proposed by the first correspondent. Active Christian piety *was* important, but not to the exclusion of faithful political engagement as the second correspondent seemed to be urging.

America's Christian heritage, especially its Protestant Christian heritage, has tended to oscillate between political non-involvement and political over-involvement. My prediction for the future is that these contrasting styles will probably continue to dominate American religious life—that is, the tendency to treat the next election as the apocalypse and the tendency to dismiss the next election as irrelevant to genuine Christian life. But alongside these dominant tendencies, I think it is possible to glimpse many signs of a better kind of Christian politics that may open up even further in the days ahead.

These signs come in many varieties. In my view, it is all to the good that the principled Christian stand against abortion rights and the abortion industry has broadened out in many parts of the United States into support for prenatal, family counseling, and adoption services. In other words, the necessary protest against the culture of death is being matched by far-seeing understanding of what is entailed by a culture of life. I see another sign of hope in the number of Christian advocacy groups that urge their supporters to *think* through the meaning of political responsibility, to broaden political engagement beyond a single-issue mentality, to use partisanship rather than being used by it. I am thinking of organizations like Evangelicals for Social Action, Bread for the World, and the Center for Public Justice, but there are many others as well. Such groups are pointing the way ahead on a number of political issues that are as clearly a part of responsible Christian politics as the pro-life movement. But these are issues where the moral terrain is more complicated—issues like public education, inner-city and rural poverty, access to health insurance, voter apathy, the leverage of economic power and, above all, race relations. I am encouraged not because any of these groups have succeeded in "solving" such intractable problems but because they are bringing to bear careful Christian reflection and the hard labor of public education at a wiser, more self-conscious and more intrinsically biblical level than has ever been done in American history to this date.

Comparative Christianity

My last faltering effort at prediction concerns the relation of the United States' Christian communities with Christian communities in the rest of the world. My sense is that, even with all of the relative vitality in America's churches, the public place of Christianity in this country will be increasingly marginalized in the years ahead, even as it has been increasingly marginalized by degrees over the course of the century just passed. What I mean is that, while many signs of hope will break from American Christian communities, it is less and less likely that Christian influences will ever again dominate the country's great shapers of culture as the churches and Christian agencies did through much of the nineteenth century and into the twentieth. The popular media, elite print culture, mass circulation print culture, higher education, and the nation's economic life all seem to me drifting *in the main* away from Christian values. "In the main" is an important qualification, since the general drift toward secularism or multicultural pluralism does not, and probably will not, rule out many opportunities for faithful Christian agency in precisely these spheres of life. Yet my sense is that none of these spheres will in the near future be *converted* to Christ and the spread of his kingdom. If my supposition is correct, however, it means that Christians in the United States will be coming to experience the world as almost all Christian believers outside the U.S. actually experience the world. The burgeoning numbers of Christian believers in China, India, Africa, and Latin America are not, for the most part, culturally or socially dominant. Often they are found fairly far down the scale of power and influence.

If this analysis is correct, American believers in the twenty-first century will have many opportunities for the very best kind of cross-national and cross-cultural fellowship with believers in other parts of the world. American Christian communities will probably continue for a very long time to be much wealthier than almost all Christian communities in other parts of the world. But if American believers acknowledge and even embrace their own marginality, they will emerge into an unusual place. To be sure, it will be a place of mourning—for the ruined relics of Western Christian civilization that litter our cultural landscape testify to the loss of great treasures. But it could also be a place of significant joy—for the existential knowledge that we, like our Christian brothers and sisters in the rest of the world, are a *pilgrim* people could be a bracing tonic.

Many of the significant developments of twentieth-century history point in the direction of a pilgrim status for the American churches. The growing numbers of churches, denominations, and parachurch agencies, as well as the growing diversity of ethnic churches, make close cooperation among churches increasingly problematic. The conservative, evangelical, Pentecostal, fundamentalist, and charismatic churches that are growing for the most part lack the instincts of civilization that were so much a part of the older mainline Protestant churches. Increased opportunities for Catholic-Protestant engagement are, in my view, a godsend, but they also speak to a great deal of internal disarray among both Catholics and Protestants. And as refreshing as the recent emphasis on the Holy Spirit can be, Pentecostal, charismatic, and Spirit-emphasizing churches have never been as effective at the tasks of Christian civilization as the older liturgical, hierarchical, or word-centered churches. We may face, in other words, a situation where the United States experiences *both* increasing Christian vitality *and* decreasing Christian influence. If that were to be the case, it could be a useful development, especially if it brought America's Christian communities closer to the Christian communities of the rest of the world, where a similar set of conditions is likely to prevail for some time to come.

My faltering efforts at prediction are now done. As a historian, I look back over the twentieth century with roughly equal measures of surprise, despair, and hope. However foolish my thoughts about the specific shape of the future may be, I see no reason not to maintain the same attitudes toward the days to come:

- surprise for what God's people may do that no one thought they ever could do
- despair for what God's people may do that they never should have done
- most of all hope—not so much in God's people but in the loving God who in the person of His Son will open His arms throughout the twenty-first century just as wide as He has done for millennia past to all who are weary and heavy laden and who would find their rest in Him.

Notes

1. See David Martin, *Tongues of Fire: The Explosion of Protestantism in Latin America* (Oxford: Blackwell, 1990); and Walter J. Hollenweger, *Pentecostalism: Origins and Developments Worldwide* (Peabody, Mass.: Hendrickson, 1997).

2. See Edith Blumhofer, *Restoring the Faith: The Assemblies of God, Pentecostalism, and American Culture* (Urbana: University of Illinois Press, 1993); and for the emphases of the early movement, Grant Wacker, *Heaven Below: Early Pentecostals and American Culture* (Cambridge, Mass.: Harvard University Press, 2001).

3. The most substantial theological critique is found in the work of David F. Wells, for example, *No Place for Truth, or, Whatever Happened to Evangelical Theology* (Grand Rapids, Mich.: Eerdmans, 1993), and *Losing Our Virtue: Why the Church Must Recover Its Moral Vision* (Grand Rapids, Mich.: Eerdmans, 1998).

4.. Kenneth B. Bedell, ed., *1997 Yearbook of American and Canadian Churches* (Nashville, Tenn.: Abingdon, for the National Council of Churches, 1997).

5. See Kenneth R. Samples, "The Recent Truth about Seventh-day Adventists," *Christianity Today* (5 Feb. 1990): 18–21; Doug LeBlanc, "The Worldwide Church of God: Resurrected into Orthodoxy," *Christian Research Journal* (Winter 1996): 6–7, 44–45.

6. Martin, *Tongues of Fire,* 206. This important book explains why America's important earlier forms of Protestantism (Puritanism and Methodism) did not transport easily to Latin America, but why the third (Pentecostalism) is doing so with a vengeance.

7. Charles Marsh, *God's Long Summer: Stories of Faith and Civil Rights* (Princeton, N.J.: Princeton University Press, 1997).

8. See Ward Clark Roof and William McKinney, *American Mainline Religion* (New Brunswick, N.J.: Rutgers University Press, 1987) and the six-volume examination of the Presbyterians edited by John M. Mulder, Louis B. Weeks, and Milton J. Coalter, *The Presbyterian Presence: The Twentieth-Century Experience* (Louisville, Ky.: Westminster/John Knox, 1990–1992).

9. For a tour, see Randall Balmer, *Mine Eyes Have Seen the Glory: A Journey into the Evangelical Subculture in America* (New York: Oxford University Press, 1989).

10. See Lyman Kellstedt and John C. Green, "The Mismeasure of Evangelicals," *Books & Culture: A Christian Review* (Jan.–Feb. 1996): 14–15, and James L. Guth, John C. Green, Corwin E. Smidt, and Lyman A. Kellstedt, "Partisan Religion: Analyzing the 2000 Election," *Christian Century* (March 21–28, 2001): 18–20.

11. On this subject, an important discussion was sparked by Dean M. Kelley, *Why Conservative Churches Are Growing* (New York: Harper & Row, 1972).

12. On Packer's own influential career as an evangelical spokesman, see Mark A. Noll, "J. I. Packer and the Shaping of American Evangelicalism" in *Doing Theology for the People of God: Studies in Honor of J. I. Packer,* Donald Lewis and Alister McGrath, eds. (Downers Grove, IL: InterVarsity Press, 1996), 191–206.

13. J. I. Packer, review of *The Born-Again Catholic* (Locust, Valley, NY: Living Flame Press, 1980) in *Eternity* (Dec. 1983): 92.

14. Theodore C. Sorensen, *Kennedy* (New York: Harper & Row, 1965), 188–95, 357–65; Marshall Frady, *Billy Graham: A Parable of American Righteousness* (Boston: Little, Brown, 1979), 446.

15. John B. Sheerin, "American Catholics and Ecumenism," in *Contemporary Catholicism,* 75–78. Some of the texts from these discussions from the 1970s and early 1980s are collected in Harding Meyer and Lukas Vischer, eds., *Growth in Agreement: Reports and Agreed Statements of Ecumenical Conversations on a World Level* (New York: Paulist, 1984).

16. The results of these dialogues published by Augsburg Press include *The Status of the Nicene Creed as Dogma of the Church* (1965), *One Baptism for the Remission of Sins* (1966), *The Eucharist as Sacrifice* (1967), *Eucharist and Ministry* (1970), *Papal Primacy and the Universal Church* (1974), *Teaching Authority and Infallibility in the Church* (1980), and *The One Mediator, The Saints, and Mary* (1992).

17. A good treatment of the role of Catholicism in the fall of communism in Poland and Czechoslovakia is George Weigel, *The Final Revolution: The Resistance Church and the Collapse of Communism* (New York: Oxford University Press, 1992); for a responsible effort at biography, see Wiegel's *Witness to Hope: The Biography of Pope John Paul II* (New York: Harper Collins, 1999).

18. Quoted in *Christian Century* (June 30–July 7, 1999): 670. For cautious analysis by an American evangelical, see Douglas A. Sweeney, "Taming the Reformation," *Christianity Today* (Jan. 10, 2000): 63–65.

19. See, for example, Thomas A. Tweed, *Our Lady of the Exile: Diasporic Religion at a Cuban Catholic Shrine in Miami* (New York: Oxford University Press, 1997).

20. Lewis C. Perry, *Intellectual Life in America: A History* (Chicago. University of Chicago Press, 1989.)

Chapter Three

Christophobia and the American Future

Marvin Olasky

January 29, 2001, was a day historians will relish, and not only because it was the day after a dull Super Bowl. On that day President Bush met at the White House with about thirty religious leaders and one minor historian to demonstrate his commitment to ending discrimination against strongly religious organizations. He then strode into the ornate Indian Treaty room to announce to the press formation of his Office of Faith-Based and Community Initiatives.

I'm not so blasé as to be indifferent to meetings in the White House or with George W. Bush, but they don't give me goose bumps any more. I do believe that Mr. Bush is a good man who is a very good president and may become a great one—but he is a human being, not a god. What made January 29 a great day was that it was so long in coming, and that it had arrived against great odds. Suffering New Englanders will understand this analogy: It was as if the Boston Red Sox, who have not won a World Series since 1918, became the champions.

I recently ran across a good book from two decades past, Lynn Buzzard and Samuel Ericsson's *The Battle for Religious Liberty.* They wrote about how in 1980 the mayor of Los Angeles said that private *homes* could no longer host Bible studies. Similar comments came from government officials in Massachusetts and Florida. Believers in God were on the defensive

MARVIN OLASKY, the author of thirteen books, including *Compassionate Conservatism*, edits the weekly newsmagazine *World,* serves as senior fellow at the Acton Institute for the Study of Religion and Liberty, and teaches courses on Journalism and Religion at the University of Texas at Austin.

everywhere in America two decades ago, and the cocky self-description of one group as the Moral Majority didn't fool many people.

The same skepticism was evident concerning efforts to reform poverty fighting in America during the 1980s. A mighty fortress was the welfare state, and welfare rolls tended to increase in good times or bad. Nor was a speech I gave in 1989 about compassionate conservatism particularly optimistic. It ended on a wistful note: Maybe someday we will break free of the government welfare monolith.

I've spent the past dozen years learning and then teaching about compassionate conservatism, but I often wondered whether we could have a breakthrough. Every spring I would ask my wife, "Do you think the Red Sox will win the World Series this year?" Every spring I would wonder whether the success of many faith-based programs, generally based in Christianity, would overcome the Christophobia that makes some folks believe that the only thing worse than those programs failing would be to have them succeed. That's because success would reveal the power of God, a power much feared.

I had originally planned to present a general lecture about Christophobia in American life. The debate over President Bush's faith-based initiative, however, presents a terrific case study of the phenomenon, as well as an indication of how things have changed during the past two decades and especially during the past two years. The question is no longer whether Bible studies can be in private homes; it's whether they can be in public places like government offices. Now, those who say "Don't talk about God, and don't run an antipoverty program as if God existed" are on the defensive.

I don't say that lightly, nor do I think that because Christians and conservatives now have the ball that we're on our way to scoring a touchdown. We're still back on our own twenty-yard line, and while the country and our political leaders have changed in the past two decades, the liberal Washington press corps has not. Its captains are ready to fight anyone who will pull the razor wire off the top of the wall of separation between church and state. And so I want to talk tonight about answers to Christophobic questions poised by many reporters: Will you allow proselytizing? Won't loose lips regarding God sink the First Amendment? Will churches corrupt government?

Fear of Proselytizing

I'll start with the journalistic question from the left most frequently asked so far: Under President Bush's faith-based initiative, will groups that proselytize be eligible for government funding? The public relations tendency is to calm the journalists' concern with a "no how, no way" response. But it's not that simple.

Since I've already made a football analogy, I'll continue in that wayward tendency by mentioning the problem of the forward pass. Back-to-basics football coaches tend to frown on it because three things can happen when a quarterback throws the ball: completion, incomplete pass, interception. Two of the three are bad. The same can be said about proselytizing. To some the word connotes forced religious conversion. To others it means offering bribes to say some religious words or engage in some ritual. Two possible definitions are bad. But proselytizing can also suggest a mode of discussion that leads to a free, informed choice.

Here's a bit of history: The word "proselyte" emerged in Greek and Latin 1,800 years ago as a term for a person converting to Judaism. "Proselytize," a word that first appeared in 1679, means to induce a person to convert to one's faith. What kind of inducement? The pressure of force is the worst. In Russia under the tsars, Jews were sometimes drafted into the army and forced to undergo baptism, as if that made a person a Christian.

That's the image some folks have of proselytizing, and it's not surprising. British historian Herbert Butterfield offered my favorite definition of "history" about half a century ago: "History is a record of man's universal sin." There's plenty of it to go around. When the Turks a century ago were putting down an Armenian rebellion, in at least one instance captured Armenians were lined up and asked whether they worshiped "Christ or Allah." Those who answered "Christ" received a sword thrust to the gut.

A second type of inducement, also bad, is the material inducement offered as a payoff for making a profession of faith. Missionaries in Asia once warned of the danger of encouraging what they called "rice Christians," those who might say anything so as to get a bowl of rice. What if Christians running a homeless shelter today tied the provision of food and shelter, "three hots and a cot," to saying some supposedly magic words about Jesus? That brand of proselytizing would also be labeled both dumb and disgraceful, and rightly so.

Happily, we don't have that type of proselytizing in America. What's common at faith-based groups are counselors who tell discouraged clients that a wonderful God created them in His own image, so that there is something wonderful about the clients themselves. The counselors also talk about how belief in God is good not only for themselves but for others as well. I teach a course called "Journalism and Religion" at the University of Texas and regularly bring in Muslims, Jews, Christians, Buddhists, Hindus, and others for the class to interview. Each interviewee proselytizes in the third sense of the word. He lays out arguments why his belief is right. He reasons with students who ask questions. He invites them to attend worship services and discussions.

Christians in particular are called to engage in that third type of proselytizing, also known as evangelizing. The last command of Jesus in the gospel according to Mark is to "go and make disciples of all nations." Christians call that "the great commission." Throughout most of American history evangelical Protestants and Catholics have run homeless shelters in large American cities, offering both material and spiritual food. Individuals have not been forced in, but those who came were expected to listen to some kind of a sermon.

I've listened to sermons at homeless shelters and feeding programs in Chicago, New York, and Washington, and in Pennsylvania, Indiana, Oklahoma, and Texas as well. Some have been good. Some have been bad. Most have been short. None of the listeners has ever been forced to say anything. Those sermons are as much an impediment to freedom of conscience as bathing suits are to freedom of swimming. Sure, some "naturalists" think that all beaches should be nude ones, but for most people it's natural to wear a swimsuit at a beach. For most people it's natural to hear a sermon at a Christian shelter. As long as secular alternatives are available, why is this terrible?

Whenever we hear someone praise or (more likely) condemn proselytizing, we should ask, "What do you mean by that?" Some people think of proselytizing as badgering a person until he gives in. That's rude and wrong. Other people don't like the idea of ever encountering, or having others encounter, unfashionable religious ideas. But the freedom to proselytize in that sense is part of our liberty, and it makes our land sweet. If a journalist or U.S. senator starts blazing against proselytizing, defenders of President Bush's initiative should not become defensive but should stay on offense. Since when in America should we be afraid of freedom of speech and a free exchange of ideas?

Constitutional Questions

Critics from the left will often bring up the First Amendment at this point, but that amendment is designed to protect religious debate. The British during colonial days tried to forbid critiques of the established, government-preferred Anglican denomination. Some Anglicans in Virginia even thrust whips down the throats of Baptist preachers and in the process infuriated young James Madison, who condemned the "diabolic, hell-conceived principle of persecution." His anger fifteen years later led to sixteen powerful words of the first amendment: "Congress shall make no law respecting an establishment of religion, or prohibiting the free exercise thereof. . . ."

That initial clause, in the language of two centuries ago, means that Congress shall not establish—give preference to—a religion. The second clause means that people who believe in God should be able to carry through on that belief not just for an hour on Sunday but all through the week. Let me emphasize this: "An establishment of religion" means designating one religion as the one that receives preference and direct funding from government, to the exclusion of other religious views. Madison assured members of Congress debating the First Amendment in 1789 that it would not cut off government from support from religion generally. The amendment was needed, he said, because "the people feared that one sect might obtain a preeminence."

Even Thomas Jefferson, who as president wrote in a private letter those famous words about "a wall of separation" between church and state, signed treaties with Indian tribes that included the provision of federal money to build churches and support clergymen. Jefferson even extended three times an act that designated federal lands for "the sole use of Christian Indians and the Moravian Brethren missionaries for use in civilizing the Indians and promoting Christianity." Jefferson, more than any of the other founders, wanted a wall, but even he did not put broken glass on top of it.

The U.S. Supreme Court for a century and a half assumed a friendly relationship between church and state. Famed Supreme Court Justice Joseph Story even wrote in 1833 that the First Amendment allowed "Christianity . . . to receive encouragement from the state, so far as not incompatible with the private rights of conscience, and the freedom of religious worship." Jefferson's wall metaphor languished for years until the Supreme

Court pulled it out of the historical dust in 1947, but even then "separation of church and state" did not mean separation of people who believe in God from any governmental connection.

Even one of the leading Supreme Court secularists, Justice William O. Douglas, wrote in 1952 that if church and state were always separated, "the state and religion would be aliens to each other—hostile, suspicious and even unfriendly." Douglas's most famous sentence, when he wrote that majority opinion in *Zorach v. Clausen*, was, "We are a religious people whose institutions presuppose a Supreme Being." But he went on to emphasize "the religious nature of our people" and the need for an understanding that "accommodates the public service to their spiritual needs. . . . [We] find no constitutional requirement which makes it necessary for government to be hostile to religion and to throw its weight against efforts to widen the effective scope of religious influence."

Other justices have reasoned similarly. In the 1960s, Justice Arthur Goldberg warned of the need to avoid "a brooding and pervasive devotion to the secular and a passive, or even active, hostility to the religious." In the 1970s Chief Justice Warren Burger played with the "wall of separation" metaphor, writing that "the line of separation, far from being 'a wall,' is a blurred, indistinct and variable barrier." In the 1980s now–Chief Justice William Rehnquist, dissenting in *Wallace v. Jaffree*, wrote that "The 'wall of separation between church and State' is a metaphor based on bad history, a metaphor which has proved useless as a guide to judging. It should be frankly and explicitly abandoned."

Rehnquist was in the minority, especially in his strict constructionist philosophy. (He noted that "the greatest injury of the 'wall' notion is its mischievous diversion of judges from the actual intentions of the drafters of the Bill of Rights.") Nevertheless, in recent years the Supreme Court has gone a long way to opening up schools to a variety of religious influences and messages, as long as the government is not giving preference to one. The barrier is more blurred than ever, and only spinmeisters can claim otherwise.

Given the blur, I believe the key question that the Supreme Court might consider is not whether the Bush attitude of welcoming all religious groups should be allowed, but whether it must be allowed. A strong argument can be made that we have been violating for three or four decades now the First Amendment's emphasis on a level playing field. I'll give you two ways that we have done that.

First, within churches, one longstanding debate has pitted supporters of the ministry of the deed—"just feed people"—versus defenders of holistic ministry: feed, yes, but also present verbally who Christ is. Catholic Charities, Lutheran Social Services, and some other groups advocate the former. I believe that the latter is more in keeping with the position of Christ: After all, he fed people only twice, and both times after he had taught them.

Regardless of which side you're on, here's the important constitutional point: This is a theological debate. Should the federal government be putting its thumb on the scale by preferring one religious view and redlining the other? That's what happens when bureaucrats say, "OK, theologically liberal Christians, you can have free expression of your faith within governmental programs by feeding people. Theological conservatives, you need to be gagged, because adding verbal explanation to material help is not allowed."

The second way our government has shown bias is by seeing things in an opposite way to that of the boy in the famous story about the emperor's new clothes. You'll remember that the emperor is actually naked but everyone except the honest little boy pretends that he is dressed. Here, our tendency has been to pretend that government offices have no religious clothes if they do not endorse Christianity, Judaism, or some other theistic faith. Actually, they do, and even if the government were to eliminate grants to Catholic Charities or Lutheran Social Services, that would not solve the First Amendment program.

Why? Look at the secondary standard dictionary definition of "religion": "a cause, principle, or system of beliefs held to with ardor and faith." In that sense, the materialism that dominates government programs—the idea that people are wholly material and that satisfying material needs solves the problem—is also a religion, and one we have now established. If you think that's stretching the First Amendment, I would draw your attention to some of the debates of the 1780s. Those voting for the First Amendment knew of the danger of establishing secularism, and they made it clear, as Benjamin Huntington of Connecticut and others stipulated, that the government should not "patronize"—give patronage to—atheists in practice.

Practical Implications

I've talked about the importance of allowing a liberty-preserving type of proselytizing and of discarding the notion that the First Amendment is hostile to religion. I also want to deal with what will happen if we get either of these two things wrong and thereby kick out evangelical groups from participation in any governmental programs. Here's my concern: I've known some enormously self-sacrificing atheists, but for the most part people who volunteer for the time-intensive, week-in-week-out, one-to-one mentoring of needy individuals do so because of faith in God.

Typically, such individuals believe that God wants them to persevere in such self-sacrificial loving of their neighbors as themselves. Typically, many also believe that their faith in God has changed them, and that the greatest gift they can offer to those they are helping is to convey that understanding of how God changes lives. If government officials tell such volunteers that any kind of federal program funding means they cannot speak about what is most important to them and to the future of their clients, those volunteers will not participate. If that happens, the programs will work poorly, or not at all.

I had lunch recently with a good man, a Democratic state representative in Texas, who thought that it would not be hard to find volunteers to join the armies of compassion. If we're just talking about passing out food occasionally, or even tutoring a child, I think he is right. If our emphasis, though, is on finding volunteers willing to "suffer with" those in need—that's the literal definition of compassion—by coming alongside people who have messed up their lives, the task is harder. If we hope for volunteers to persevere week after week after week, for several hours every week, the task is much, much harder.

We cannot assume that marginalizing some very effective groups will have no effect on the provision of mercy. We need a strategy that understands the curve of supply-side compassion. Shutting off evangelicals or others who believe that a change in heart is more important than passing out spare change will reduce sharply the outflow of compassion.

I have confidence in how President Bush will react to attempts to redline evangelicals or any others who believe in the ministry of the word as well as the ministry of the deed. That confidence is based partly on my understanding of what he believes. It is also based on what he has said repeatedly: "We will never ask an organization to compromise its core principles and spiritual mission to get the help it needs." "Never" is a long-lasting word. I'm also confident because of how President Bush acted under pressure during the campaign. He identified Jesus as his favorite thinker and did not back down even when that angered some journalists. I also have confidence in those who are leading the Office of Faith-Based and Community Initiatives. The pressures on them are enormous.

I do not have a lot of confidence in some of the interest groups involved. Americans United for the Separation of Church and State insists that any funds religious groups receive blast a hole in the church-state "wall of separation." Sometimes it and other groups will use sweet words, such as those in an open letter to President Bush the day after he announced his faith-based initiatives. The letter included a list of complaints and the conclusion, "We look forward to working with you to remedy these Constitutional and policy defects." Such words were last heard just before a prisoner was put on the rack, then drawn and quartered.

I do not have a lot of confidence in Congress, particularly in the Senate. Not only are Democrats and Republicans narrowly divided, but also liberal Republican senators outnumber conservative Democrats. Here's where the role of the press and public opinion is crucial. The easy way to win the votes of many liberals is to give official preference to theological liberalism and thrust theological conservatism out the door. But that, as I've outlined, will be unfair, unconstitutional, and disastrous for effective poverty fighting—and for Republican political hopes.

I mention those hopes because everything in Washington has political overtones. What if compassionate conservative initiatives go through the congressional sausage grinder and end up so distorted that they create more discrimination rather than less? Within Protestantism, for example, some fundamentalists are separatists, but many of them, and many of the broader evangelicals, are transformationists. They are not merely trying to play defense and protect a church fortress. They hope that the gospel will change lives and transform a culture, both by the effect of those lives and the application of biblical principles to American life. Allies from other religions in today's culture wars also refuse to give up.

If conservative Christians, because of their emphasis on the third kind of proselytizing, are sold down the river in the course of legislative negotiations, the transformationists will be bitterly disappointed. The separatists will still see bias at work and feel alienated from political life and from those who failed to fight for them.

Christophobia

This brings me back to my initial observations about who is on offense and who is on defense in American culture right now and on what yard line the ball is placed. It astounds me that folks on the left talk as if theocrats have marched down the field to the secularists' red zone and are poised to score. American churches and other religious institutions are weak in relation to our massive government. Faith-based welfare operates largely at the margins and will continue to do so for at least the next decade, even under the most optimistic, compassionate, conservative projections.

If the United States were about to be taken over by a particular religion, we would have to ignore the supply-side considerations and other matters I have spoken of in order to protect liberty. But let's get real, and let's bulwark observation of reality with a Madisonian view of politics. In the 1780s James Madison turned conventional analysis on its head by seeing the numerous factions within a large country not as a danger but as a source of strength. Today, so many religious groups compete in the American ideological marketplace, and so many of them are critical of each other, that we have no danger of a religious cabal grabbing power.

Why do we hear so often in media and academia these fears of religion? I suspect that we're seeing rampant Christophobia, which is far more prevalent than homophobia, although you wouldn't know that from press coverage. (I checked Lexis-Nexis and found less than one reference to Christophobia, on average, over the past twenty years but over 1,000 in each recent year to homophobia.) We see it in the attacks on conservative Christians during political campaigns, and we see it regularly in Hollywood's snide depictions of Christians.

Such sarcasm trivializes the real issues. The Bible describes a true phobia—fear of God and his angels—that actually is a consuming fire for many. Virtually every scriptural angel says to those quivering in the presence of the supernatural, "Fear not." I believe that all of us are sinners and have good reason to fear a holy God, until He graciously tells us, "fear not," and even more graciously provides a way to escape His wrath. I believe that if we run from Christ we fear him all the more, because deep down we know we are throwing away our best hope. So Christophobia, unlike homophobia, is widespread.

How Christophobic has America become? Two centuries ago Americans opposed any particular denomination becoming the established religion, but they saw biblical belief underlying our entire government and social structure. Alexis de Tocqueville in the early nineteenth century noted that "Americans combine the notions of Christianity and of liberty so intimately in their minds that it is impossible to make them conceive the one without the other." But the Williamsburg Charter Survey on Religion and Public Life a decade ago found 92 percent of surveyed academics demanding a "high wall of separation" between church and state. One-third even claimed that evangelicals are "a threat to democracy."

One perceptive viewer of this bias today is not a Christian but an Orthodox Jewish rabbi. Daniel Lapin wrote in his book *America's Real War* that "The educational bureaucracy expects the state to accommodate every possible bizarre cultural mutation and lifestyle, but finds prayer at graduation an intolerable and fatal compromise of state neutrality toward religion." Phobias produce illogic. Rabbi Lapin also noted that "Those of us who venerate freedom, be we Jewish or Christian, be we religious or secularized, have no option but to pray for the health of Christianity in America. No other group possesses both the faith and the numbers sufficient to hold back the ever-encroaching, sometimes sinister, power of the state."

Christophobia in America is not primarily connected to Judaism or any other non-Christian religion: liberal Protestant churches are often the most Christophobic of all. A tough-minded evangelical presence brings with it the moral confrontation that Christ emphasized and that churches fleeing from the Gospel hope to avoid. But churches and members that have given up their heritage do have much to fear, because in God's economy it is not better to have loved and walked away than never to have loved at all. We are now understanding more about the emotional devastation known as postabortion syndrome. We need to look into postbiblical syndrome, mourning for what is lost even when smiles on the outside remain.

President Bush

I do believe that George W. Bush could be a great president because he could do for some aspects of Christophobia what Ronald Reagan did for some aspects of conservatism. President Reagan did not win over hardcore liberals, but he showed many folks in the middle that fear of conservatism was misplaced. President Bush can reduce the level of Christophobia by explaining publicly, as he did at the January 29, 2001 meeting, why it's vital to emphasize "changing lives by changing hearts."

His performance that day with the religious leaders was dynamic. Aware of the bias against religious groups, he pledged to fight it and acknowledged that his attempt to do so will "come under withering fire by some." But then came the pledge: "I promise you I will stand up for what I believe . . . an initiative and a vision that will fundamentally change our country." Some folks in the room reported on the suspicions that abound, but President Bush, while saying "I fully understand the fears of people of faith," emphasized how important it was to go on offense instead of constantly being on defense.

President Bush also spoke of person-to-person compassion, arguing that "This was the core of America. . . . Then government stepped in, and everyone said government could do it." He predicted a legal battle with those who demand that religion be banned from government premises—but, he insisted, "we'll win it." He said, "The first fight will be with the press corps," and he knew it would be hard, but he insisted: "This is the right thing to do." He showed his personal understanding of why that is the right thing to do: "I was lost and then I was found." And he knew that what is most needed is religious revival in America.

What was extraordinary here was President Bush's evident belief that religious faith is not just something to express during an hour on Sunday but also something significant for action all through the week. I think he understands that the Sabbath is the last day of the week but also the first. It's a day of rest but also a day for reloading. We've come a long way from a defensive crouch, hoping that just maybe we can have a Bible study in our home without someone calling the police.

Many people still don't realize the opportunities. The pessimistic attitude of some reminds me of a story about a man who lay dying in his bed. He suddenly smelled the aroma of his favorite chocolate chip cookies wafting up the stairs. He gathered his remaining strength. With great effort he forced himself down the stairs and gazed into the kitchen. Spread out upon platters on the kitchen table were hundreds of his favorite chocolate chip cookies. Mustering one great final effort, he threw himself toward the table. His parched lips parted; the wonderful taste of the cookie was already in his mouth, seemingly bringing him back. The aged and withered hand shakingly made its way to a cookie at the edge of the table, when it was suddenly smacked with a spatula by his wife. "Stay out of those," she said, "they're for the funeral."

We have expected funerals, but instead we see new life. The real promise of President Bush's initiatives is contained in the words that are etched on the administration building of the University of Texas at Austin, and on many similar buildings throughout the country. The sentence, from the Gospel according to John, is simple yet profound: "You shall know the truth, and the truth will set you free."

Chapter Four

Ideas That Bring Down Empires

AN EVANGELICAL CASE FOR
SCHOLARSHIP

George Marsden

Looking beyond my ideas in *The Outrageous Idea of Christian Scholarship,*
I would like to address the mission of a Christian *college* regarding the important matter of *Faith, Freedom, and the Future.*

People who think Christian scholarship is outrageous may be divided,
broadly speaking, into two camps. First there are those non-Christians
who find the idea outrageous or offensive. For modern scholars to relate
faith and learning is, as one prominent historian put it, a "loony" idea.
Many regard such scholarship as necessarily unscientific. Or they may regard it as offensive for Christians to set themselves apart as though they
have a view of things that is distinct and superior to that of other secular
or religious groups. My book is first of all a response to such critics and second provides some guidelines to Christian scholars as to how to think
about their relationship to an often hostile or suspicious mainstream
academy.

I want to talk about another group that tends to be deeply suspicious of
the idea of Christian scholarship. This group includes most American
evangelical Christians. This group is suspicious not of the *Christian* part of
the idea, but rather of the *scholarship* part. American evangelical Christians

GEORGE MARSDEN, the Francis A. McAnaney Professor of History at the University of
Notre Dame, includes among his books *Fundamentalism and American Culture, The Search for a
Christian America, Evangelicalism and Modern America, Religion and American Culture, The Secularization of the Academy, The Soul of the American University,* and *The Outrageous Idea of Christian Scholarship.*

are notoriously anti-intellectual. That is something that is not just said about us by outsiders. Insiders have also pointed out this distrust of serious intellectual pursuits. The best-known expression of this point is in Mark Noll's *The Scandal of the Evangelical Mind.* The scandal of the evangelical mind, Noll argues in essence, is that there is no evangelical mind. Evangelical Americans are extremely pragmatic. They do what works. They want to save souls or sometimes they want to organize for quick action to change the world. But they seldom take the time to build good theory or good theology for what they are doing. As one evangelical leader said to me, their operating procedure tends to be "Load, fire, aim."

Among evangelicals, Reformed and Presbyterian Christians have probably been the least given to such anti-intellectualism. We have, after all, a long tradition of formidable intellectual achievement going back to the Puritans and the Reformers. Nevertheless, I think it is safe to say that American evangelical activism and suspicions of scholarship have infected even the strongest Reformed and Presbyterian communities of today. In fact, I think that we can find some of the best evidence of such suspicions in the structures of most Christian colleges, including Reformed ones, today. Even if scholarship is *respected* in America's Christian academic institutions, it is not—if we are to look at where the money is—something that has a high priority. And remember, we are talking about the *academic* institutions—the places we might think were set aside especially to cultivate scholarship.

I would like to address the question of how the strengths of the American evangelical activist heritage and a healthy cultivation of Christian intellectual life might be combined. Notice I am not suggesting that a stronger emphasis on scholarship ought to be an *alternative* to the strengths of evangelical activism. Rather, I want you to think about how scholarship might be seen as an integral part of the evangelical mission to the world. In other words, how should the evangelistic strengths of the Protestant tradition be linked to its intellectual strengths?

The Machen Model

In thinking about this topic over the years I have been immensely helped by the insights of one of my spiritual forefathers, J. Gresham Machen. Machen was a leading Presbyterian scholar at Princeton Theological Seminary in the early decades of the twentieth century. Later he was the principal founder of Westminster Theological Seminary and the Orthodox Presbyterian Church.

Early in my career, when I was teaching at Calvin College, I ran into some of Machen's early reflections on this topic of which I had been previously unaware. It happened that during the later 1960s I visited L'Abri Fellowship in Switzerland conducted by Francis Schaeffer. Schaeffer, as you probably know, was a widely influential evangelist who spoke much of the relationship of Christian faith to contemporary culture and intellect. When I visited L'Abri I found that he had reprinted as a little pamphlet an address, titled "Christianity and Culture," that had been especially influential on him in shaping his own sense of mission. Machen had been one of Schaeffer's teachers in the 1930s. But the address that Schaeffer rediscovered had been delivered when Machen was a young teacher at a convocation at Princeton Theological Seminary in 1912.[1]

The early twentieth century was a time of church growth and enthusiasm for evangelism and missions in American Protestant churches. Young men who had chosen such a conservative seminary as Princeton were likely to have done so not so much for intellectual reasons as because of enthusiasm for evangelism that they saw as lacking at the more liberal seminaries. Their tendency, Machen knew well, was to question why they had to take so much time for rigorous learning when there was so much practical gospel work to be done, when untold numbers were perishing in their sins every day. Machen well describes such activist students as saying:

> The gospel is the sole means of escape [from the crisis of modern civilization]; let us preach it to the world while yet we may. So desperate is the need that we have no time to engage in vain babblings and old wives' fables. While we are discussing the exact location of the churches of Galatia, men are perishing under the curse of the law; while we are settling the date of Jesus's birth, the world is doing without its Christmas message.

Machen responds to such criticisms by challenging the assumption of evangelical Americans that scholarship is impractical and irrelevant to the urgent task of evangelism. On the contrary the intellectual task is an essential component of evangelism. That is because God works through *means* to bring people to himself and these means include cultural conditions that may dispose people to give the gospel a hearing. In the twentieth century, Machen observes, the intellectual obstacles to the faith seem insurmountable for many people. This is true not only for the intellectuals but also for masses of people who are shaped by prevailing cultural fashion. So Christian scholarship is not only making good use of God's creation—another good rationale—it also can provide a vital component of evangelism.

> We may preach with all the fervor of a reformer [Machen proclaims] and yet succeed only in winning a straggler here and there, if we permit the whole collective thought of the nation or of the world to be controlled by ideas which, by the resistless force of logic, prevent Christianity from being regarded as anything more than a harmless delusion.

Machen's statement is a powerful one regarding what in the title to this series is called "Faith, Freedom, and the Future." The future of Christianity, both as a message for evangelism and as a factor in civilization, is dependent, in part, on the credibility of the Christian faith. If the elites who control the media, government, business, the law, and so forth come to regard Christianity as nothing more than "a harmless delusion," then the task of the Christian evangelist or the Christian citizen will become immensely more difficult.

This brings us to the key statement of what I would like you to consider. Machen's view of the potential importance of Christian scholarship is built on a more general view about the relation of ideas to history.

> What is today a matter of academic speculation [he declares] begins tomorrow to move armies and pull down empires. In that second stage, it has gone too far to be combated; the time to stop it was when it was still a matter of impassionate debate.

Ideas and Empires

I would like you to reflect on that statement in thinking what might be the intellectual task of Christian schools. If it is true that "what is a matter of academic speculation in one era begins to move armies and pull down empires in the next," what does that mean for us?

I think there is no doubt that this basic thesis is true. The Reformation was, among other things, the outgrowth of scholars' insights. The American Revolution was in part the result of ideas that could be found on scholars' drawing boards a century earlier. The French Revolution even more dramatically was driven in part by ideologies of the preceding era of Enlightenment. Some of the best examples of the influence of ideas occurred after Machen spoke; Karl Marx's theories of the mid-nineteenth century moved countless armies and pulled down empires in our century. Turn-of-the-century speculations on racial evolution as popularized by a demonic führer led directly to the devastating havoc of the Holocaust.

Of course, many other factors, including economic, political, and ethnic, account for the rise and fall of empires or for why people adopt particular ideas. As a historian, one becomes well aware of the complexities of the relationships between human beliefs and human actions. Yet there's no denying that among those factors that steer world history is the force of ideas themselves.

So I think there is a good case for Machen's primary assertion that God works through the influential ideas in a culture and not just through individuals, families, nations, or even just through churches. Cultural conditions help dispose people to belief or disbelief. Intellectual beliefs, underlying cultural assumptions, and the like are crucial parts of those cultural conditions. So Christian scholarship can have an integral role to play in evangelism and any wider Christian mission by witnessing to the intellectual viability of Christianity in an era of intellectual skepticism and by challenging widely held assumptions that are antagonistic to the faith. That point also seems to me to be irrefutable and as crucially important today as it was at the beginning of the twentieth century.

If it were the case in the United States, as it has become the case in Great Britain and Western Europe, that the overwhelming majority of the educated classes felt that they could simply dismiss traditional Christian claims as hopelessly out-of-date fairy tales, the impact on the rest of our culture would be incalculable.

It is interesting to reflect, though, on how the situation has developed quite differently in the United States. Here the dominant voices in the educated classes have also turned against traditional Christianity, and that has had a tremendous impact in the media and the arts as well as in mainstream academia itself. So something of what Machen predicted has happened. Yet the situation here is not nearly as bad as it might be. The turn against traditional Christianity at the center of the culture has not dragged everything with it—at least not yet. The situation is more like that described in Peter Berger's memorable image that the United States is like a nation where the population is as religious as that of India but is ruled by an elite who are as secular as Swedes.

The American Case

It is worth reflecting on why the United States is different from Great Britain and Western Europe on this score and how that difference should relate to our agenda as Christian educators. There are a number of cultural factors that help account for this difference, and I will not attempt to go into all of them here. An important factor that does relate to our topic, however, is the role of ethnicity and regionalism in preserving traditional religious identities. Religion has played a vital role as a centrifugal force that resists the centripetal force of the more secularized cultural center. Southern whites, African-Americans, and many ethnic groups, such as the Scotch-Irish Presbyterians of western Pennsylvania, have maintained ethno-religious identities that were out of sync with the mainstream culture. In America the spokes of the culture do not necessarily turn with the hub.

This cultural situation has had an educational counterpart. In the United States the system of higher education has been far more decentralized than that of Western Europe. Most of this decentralized college system has been church-related and much of it still is. So there always have been pockets where Christianity has survived even within higher education.

Another major factor that academics sometimes need to appreciate more is the impact of popular evangelism in sustaining the faith at all levels, including the intellectual. The flourishing of populist free-enterprise "democratic" evangelism has long been a characteristic of North American life that has distinguished it from most of its European counterparts. It is important for scholars to remember that this popular evangelism helps build a culture that makes Christian scholarship viable as well as the reverse. Countless people have been originally brought to Christianity through strongly anti-intellectual evangelists. Billy Sunday, for instance— who was an ordained Presbyterian, by the way—is supposed to have said, "I don't know any more about theology than a jack-rabbit knows about ping-pong, but I'm on my way to glory!" Many converts of such evangelists have later become well-educated and have made powerful contributions to evangelical intellectual life.

A related factor is that not all of twentieth-century evangelism has been anti-intellectual. The "evangelical mind" has been far from what it might be, but it has not been entirely missing in action either. Evangelicals have maintained many colleges and seminaries. Today many of these have fine faculty and students and are beginning to gain recognition as competitive with some of the better secular schools. Evangelical scholars can also be found at many leading universities. Perhaps the field of philosophy provides the best example. An impressive cadre of America's leading philosophers are members of the Society for Christian Philosophers. Defective as evangelical intellectual life may be, evangelicals in the United States have been able to point to scholars whose belief and academic witness help validate their own belief.

So the situation today for evangelical scholarship is not nearly as bleak as Machen might have predicted. Even though the secular debacle in the intellectual mainstream has gone on pretty much unchecked, the whole culture has not followed. Not even the whole intellectual culture has followed. For that we need to thank—among other people—the evangelists.

A Contemporary Model: Evangelism and Scholarship

That does not lessen the point that evangelists need scholars. If anything, that is truer today than at the beginning of the twentieth century. Much more than then, we live in a culture where we constantly have to depend on the authority of experts. Most Christians, even well-educated ones, are not in a position to evaluate the plausibility of belief in the historicity of the Gospels in the light of higher criticism. Nor can they demonstrate that the intellectual warrant for traditional Christian belief is as solid as is the warrant for many of the most important things that rational people believe. Nor would they have the time to marshal historical evidence against the claim that Christianity has been, on the whole, a source of oppression in history. Nor are they in a position to sort out popular claims such as that America has until recently always been a Christian nation. Nor do they have the resources to build constructive Christian views of how best to deal with problems of poverty, racial justice, justice in business and economic life, or with principles for politics, education, media, the arts, families, and so forth. For most such questions we need people in our communities who are expert on the subject and on whom we can rely.

Furthermore, if America is a culture where the people are as pious as in

India but the cultural leaders are as secular as Swedes, one wonders how long such a balance can be maintained without the Swedes winning out. If—to take just one area of modern culture—the media are overwhelmingly controlled by the secular Swedes, one wonders how long we can continue to win the hearts and minds of upcoming generations. Who among Christians is doing an adequate job to train thoughtful people who can step into positions of cultural leadership?

Populist and fundamentalist Protestantism tends to respond to such problems with demagogues and intellectual patent medicines. So it is particularly important for the thoughtful parts of the Protestant communities to build strong centers of learning that can provide counterbalances without losing enthusiasm for the essentials of the faith.

Our basic model should be the image of the Body of Christ as in I Corinthians 12 and 13, where we recognize our dependence on each others' gifts and that the highest gift is charity. We must see the mutuality of the need of Christian communities for expert scholars and the need of expert scholars for their spiritual communities.

According to this model, scholarship is neither the highest calling in the Christian church nor its greatest need. Yet it is *one* of the essential components of the Body of Christ that needs to be cultivated. It is also important to some other essential callings. One higher calling where acquaintance with the best scholarship is especially important is in the pastoral ministry. Well-informed clergy can play especially important roles in bridging the gap between the work of professional scholars and the needs of parishioners to be able to distinguish sound teaching from unsound.

Christ, Culture, and Christian Colleges

Finally, I think that at the beginning of the twenty-first century the Christian community has a wonderful opportunity to present to the secular community an alternative to the hollowness of its mainstream education.

One of the major differences between the academic situation at the beginning of the twenty-first century and that at the beginning of the twentieth is fragmentation of the dominant culture and hence of the communities and institutions that control scholarship. American culture in 1912 was as diverse as it is today, but that diversity was not reflected in its leading educational institutions. In that setting it made sense to talk about "the whole collective thought of the nation," which seemed to Machen to be controlled by the ideas that prevailed in northeastern universities such as Harvard, Yale, Columbia, Princeton, and Johns Hopkins and a few satellites in the west. If these centers became hostile to Christianity or simply ignored it, there seemed little hope for the nation.

Today, while there are still the same dominant institutions there is little intellectual coherence at those cultural centers. Part of the problem is that the system of academic specialization, combined with faddish postmodernism, has ensured that 95 percent of academic activity, even in the humanities, is unintelligible to anyone but other academic specialists in one's own field or sub-field. Furthermore, since the 1960s the idea of the dominance of any one school of thought has been under severe attack.

As deplorable as this state of affairs may be, the positive side of it is that we face a cultural and intellectual situation that appears to be going pluralistic for the foreseeable future. This pluralistic situation provides a new moment for Christian colleges and universities of which we should be talking advantage, a moment that has opened the door for Christian and other religious perspectives to be recognized as legitimate players in the mainstream dialogue. We need to be challenging the vestigial claims to universalism of non-theistic and naturalistic schools of thought.

The crucial point is that Christians today, just as at the beginning of the twentieth century, cannot allow the dominant thought of the nation to be controlled by ideas that are alien to Christianity. In the pluralistic setting we find ourselves in today, we are on the verge of effectively making this point. We are on the verge of gaining wide recognition that it is inconsistent for mainstream cultural leaders to claim that the best intellectual life must be uniform in its commitment to exclusively naturalistic views of things. On similar grounds we should also challenge the other widespread assumption of both modern and postmodern thought—the assumption that humans are the creators of their own reality. For such challenges to be effectively made, however, Christian communities will have to build first-rate intellectual centers where Christian scholars can work on such issues.

The important point to underscore is that the cultural fragmentation of today is not simply intellectual: it is also communal and institutional. This institutional fragmentation provides some of the most significant opportunities that should be shaping the agendas of those who head Christian education institutions. We should be taking advantage of this golden opportunity. In this pluralistic environment we should be building strong communities that support first-rate Christian scholarship.

So Christian colleges have an important role to play as centers that provide the opportunity for at least some faculty and students to engage in rigorous intellectual inquiring in order to provide alternative models for shaping American cultural ideals.

This is no simple task. For such alternatives to develop, schools will have to include true intellectual centers. Yet many pressures work against intellectual pursuits. Even at schools like Notre Dame and Duke, people complain about the anti-intellectualism among the students. So this is not simply an evangelical Christian problem. Colleges do a lot of other important things as well as cultivating the life of the mind. Yet *at least one of the things they do* should be to cultivate the life of the mind at the highest level. To recognize that the highest intellectual goals should be included among the things a Christian college supports is an implication of recognizing the principle of diversity of gifts. Yet a vigorous intellectual life does not develop at a college just automatically. It needs to be cultivated. Cultivating it requires leadership with great vision and willingness to commit resources to that vision. For one thing, it seems to me, faculty are greatly overworked at most schools and need more time and opportunity to develop vital Christian visions on their disciplines. To change that will take real vision and commitment of resources.

I realize that there are pressures in a hundred other directions to take a college's resources. Most of those other directions are legitimate and many, like excellence in teaching or cultivating a healthy spiritual community, are essential. The importance of a wide variety of programs and emphases needs to be recognized as consistent with the principle of the diversity of gifts. Yet that same principle demands that a strong commitment to scholarship be among the *essential* priorities. If Christian colleges are not providing for this dimension of the church's life, who else is going to? Further, I think there is a strong case, as I have been arguing, that Christian academic mission is a matter of high calling. It is also a matter of seizing an opportunity. We are in a cultural situation today in which there is a great need for alternative education from Christian perspectives that is academically competitive with the best schools in the nation. For that to happen, some visionary Christians will have to take advantage of the opportunity.

Notes

1. The address was originally published as J. Gresham Machen, "Christianity and Culture," *Princeton Theological Review* XI (January 1913): 1–15.

Chapter Five

When Faith Meets Politics

WHAT DOES IT MEAN TO TAKE
WASHINGTON, D.C., SERIOUSLY?

Jean Bethke Elshtain

Take Washington, D.C., seriously? If opinion surveys are any guide, the responses are likely to fall into one of two categories. Either: You've got to be kidding. Or: Take Washington, D.C., seriously? You bet I do. You know the old saw, don't you? The one about the most feared sentence in the English language being, "Hello, I'm from the government and I've come to help you." Thanks, but no thanks.

Political Involvement Reconsidered

I understand this attitude but I lament it, at least in part. I do believe that skepticism about the aims and claims of the sovereign state is the beginning of political wisdom, but it is only a beginning. If we begin and end with skepticism, we invite a thorough-going withdrawal from politics and that is both a pity and a shame. A pity because Christians are bidden to act as salt and light of the world. And if the salt has lost its savor, then what? A pity because we have a responsibility to act in common together toward cherished ends—and by that I don't mean conniving at getting the most advantageous tax break or the like but, rather, those ends that only the experience of living together with others affords us. Scripture warns us about making an idol of any limited human configuration, whether families or

JEAN BETHKE ELSHTAIN, Laura Spelman Rockefeller Professor of Social and Political Ethics at the University of Chicago, serves as Co-chair of the Pew Forum on Religion and Public Life. Her sixteen books include *Democracy on Trial* and *The Necessity of Politics*.

states. But from the strength that membership in the body of Christ on earth affords, we are called to go into the world, a pilgrim people, and to do what we can to protect and to defend—and I will cast this in today's dominant political language—a vision of human rights that most comports with our understanding of persons as intrinsically social and as dignified, created in the image of God.

Some say that politics is the worst possible way to protect these goods, particularly a politics that has as its focal point Washington, D.C., that great imperial city, that seething vortex of power and privilege. I suggest that we think again and I ask you to walk along with me for the next half hour or so as I try to make a limited claim on behalf of politics, including the politics that culminates in our nation's capital. I tell my students from time to time: you might not be interested in politics, but politics is interested in you. Whether you like it or not, you—all of you, but I address myself most especially to the students here today—are the subjects of politics. St. Augustine taught us, in effect, that we are always in the empire, always in a political configuration of some sort. Any other possibility awaits the end-time. So what is our stance vis-à-vis this politics? Do we ignore it utterly and wish it away? That is wishful thinking of a sort that can become, and all too often has been, utterly corrupting: think, if you will, of those "good Germans" who said in the aftermath of World War II: "But we were not political. What happened was terrible but there was nothing we could have done." We do not accept such demurrals at face value and for good reason, one being that we have the life and witness of Dietrich Bonhoeffer before us, that twentieth-century martyr to the theology of the cross who said that the Christian must stand with those being hunted, haunted, wounded, and destroyed, the least among us at any given point in time, the bleeding brothers and sisters of Jesus Christ. We do not accept such demurrals because we have before us the story of the village of Le Chambon sur Lignon, a Protestant commune not in Germany but in a kind of extension of it—occupied France—that, to the man, woman, and child, opened its doors to hounded Jewish refugees from Nazi Germany, protected and succored these wounded and helped them to escape to neutral territory. When asked what moral philosophy drove them to such dangerous deeds of goodness, the Chambonnais simply said it was an obligation of neighbor-love, that when a starving, frightened person knocks on your door you are bidden to say, "Come in, and again, come in." Politics is most definitely interested in you. How do you respond?

Freedom and Responsibility

I would argue that the greater our civic freedoms, the more expansive our responsibilities. We have wider scope for action. But we find that the overwhelming majority of college students today—some 73 percent in fact—are not interested in voting or taking part in politics, according to a report in the January 12, 2000, *New York Times;* indeed only 25 percent said they would consider time in politics even as 64 percent indicated they would consider spending some of their lives working in education and 63 percent claimed that they would work for a nonprofit group. Many of the students who expressed most vehemently a disdain for politics also said they did want to give their time to help the homeless, to tutor children, and to clean up polluted streams—but they didn't regard this as political. Many of the students interviewed offered what the *Times* called a "caustic view" of politics. Why? Politics, they said, was negative and hypocritical—more or less in this vein.

Here we have some good news and some bad news. The good news is the preparedness to put one's shoulders to the wheel in behalf of service to others. The bad news is that politics is not seen as furthering such "common good" ends and aims but, rather, standing in the way of such. This latter view takes skepticism of state power, the beginning of political wisdom, and makes it the whole as the skepticism turns into cynicism. This is unfortunate. For politics is the primary way we, in a pluralistic society, have of engaging those who are similar to us in so many ways—they, too, are human persons with human desires and fears—but who are different in so many other ways—by religious commitment, ethnic background, race region, all the many ways people can differ one from the other. Politics is the best way limited creatures like ourselves have found to negotiate these differences, not by hiding them and effacing them but by making them manifest in a way that permits such differences to remain as distinctions but not to turn into destructive divisions.

In a book called *Democracy on Trial,* published in 1995, I argued that we were in danger of losing democratic civil society because we had come to spurn those institutional forms and matrices that enable us to negotiate our differences and to mediate them in civil and political ways. I am all for what we usually call "volunteer work," but how do we sustain such engagements over the long haul? Our churches do much of the civic heavy lifting here. But what happens in D.C. helps to determine whether or not such work will be assisted in some way from the centers of power or blocked. How government helps to order economic life, for example, determines something quite basic: how many hours a day a person has to spend in the labor force. For government regulates matters such as length of the work day, minimum wage, whether or not there is a lopsided tax burden borne by some (married couples with children, for example) compared to others, whether or not there are lopsided benefits that flow to some by comparison to others, on and on. Issues of fair employment, housing, opportunity, whether a child-rearing couple lives on the razor's edge of social and economic catastrophe, whether or not the elderly cower in isolation and penury—much, not all, but much of this flows from what government, which acts, after all, in all our names whether we like it or not, is doing or not doing, as the case may be.

The early Christians had to conjure with this matter of whether to engage or to withdraw. St. Augustine, in his famous discussion of whether or not a Christian should take on the vocation of the judge, given the miseries attendant upon that vocation, argued that surely we were obliged in such matters, that we were not to evade or to avoid such responsibilities to and for that "empire" into which we had been thrust and which always pressed in on us from all sides. There are many reasons for our current civic desuetude. I want to reference one that is a really lousy reason and argue that Christians, above all, are called to repudiate the reasoning that goes into arguments from what is usually called "self interest" or, more colloquially, looking out for number one, the favorite American pasttime at present.

There is a direct relationship between the atrophy of our civic habits and the runaway triumph of a view of rights that construes rights as a way we have found to turn whatever we want into a claim on a body politic that we then spurn when it makes any direct claims on our time and attention. Our dominant image of the rights-bearing individual is precisely that—an individual, sovereign, free-standing—rather than a person construed in the image of God, relational therefore and before God not at all sovereign. We think of rights as possessions. But rights historically were a person's way of underscoring a God-given dignity that no configuration of power could take away and that no configuration of power should violate. Rights located us in a world of others rather than pitting us against one another in relationships of suspicion and competitive self-interest. As this more social understanding of rights withered, our civic habits also went into hiding.

We abandoned the ground of human personhood and occupied the ground of sovereign individualism. This is reflected in so many ways, including a weakening in the ties that bind in our religious communities as well. Religious entrepreneurialism now holds sway and individualistic forms of "spiritualism" are embraced by contrast to membership that binds us to one another and makes claims on us. One reason, I believe, that we are so hostile toward Washington is that we feel so powerless when we think of such forbidding concentrations of power. One reason we feel so powerless is that we see ourselves as standing alone—all alone with our rights, so to speak. We lose the strength that membership provides—a strength that helps us to persevere over the long haul, as communicants of our churches and as citizens of our polity.

Realism and Responsibility

In his important book *Reinhold Niebuhr and Christian Realism,* Robin Lovin offers up a defense of politics from a Christian realist perspective he associates with Niebuhr and with Augustine. It is not, therefore, a view that gives politics primacy among human activities but it is a view that, recognizing the inescapability of politics, calls upon us to engage the world of politics faithfully. How so? Here is his argument, one that I would like to associate myself with in large part. Lovin reasons thus: Christians are in a world with people who share that world but who may not share their faith, or not share it fully if we are thinking about the multiplicity of ways people locate themselves as "Christians." Politics confronts us with intransigent "otherness," people with their own opinions who are just as indefatigable in expressing those opinions as we may be in expressing our own. Politics requires that I "respond to this other in some concrete way, modifying my practices and maybe even my beliefs in ways that take this specific otherness into account." Politics is a world of compromise, for example, not as a sense of sordid complicity in awful things but as a kind of co-promising: I will do this as you do this and together we will each get something of what we find valuable, important, maybe even essential to our well-being. Politics is a world of conflicts and oppositions and that, too, may make us—in today's overused vocabulary—uncomfortable. Well, our Lord surely did a good bit to create major discomfiture. Why should Christians, of all people, shun the tough issues that are bound to raise hackles? We have been so overtaken by a sentimentalized notion of compassion—as never saying anything to make anyone else uncomfortable—that we have forgotten how to be faithful witnesses. St. Augustine, again, is a vital voice here: Neighbor-love also invites loving reproof and correction and, correlatively, means we open ourselves to such as well.

We do not know, in advance of actually engaging with others, how and in what ways we will be called upon, in Augustinian language, to press them and the ways they, in turn, will press us. This is a deeply dialogical and dialectical business. Others, in a sense, supplement our necessarily partial and incomplete perspectives: We are finite, not infinite, after all. We are not omniscient. We can know only so much and the "so much" we know may be different from the "so much" others have to offer us. Think, for example, of that process of social learning that made all of us mightily uncomfortable: the civil rights movement. The order of de jure segregation was what Augustine would call a "false peace," a peace of disordered passions and injustice. Disturbing the peace was the only way to alter that terrible situation. The churches were central disturbers but to get changes in the law and enforcement of those changes required politics.

Surely the fight against segregation was an expression of the great wisdom that ye shall know the truth and the truth shall set you free: the truth of a civic brotherhood and sisterhood, in this instance, and a vision of a human political community that more closely comports with Christian understanding of our creation in God's image, our dignity as persons. To be sure, the realization of this vision is bound to be flawed and imperfect—because we are—but that is no reason to flee from the engagement. Politics is a world of engagement with, and within, limits, yes. But politics is also called, again in Lovin's words, to gather together persons within a "particular geographical area and to create a 'workable community' out of this diverse human material." Augustine struggled with how best to define this community. He rejected the definition of civic life offered up by Scipio as quoted by Cicero, namely, the conclusion that a people is a "multitude united in association by a common sense of right and a community of interest." This is a penurious understanding, Augustine claims, and he goes on to offer up his alternative, one in which love of God and love of neighbor move center stage: "A people is the association of a multitude of rational beings united by a common agreement on the objects of their love."

It follows that to "observe the character of a people we must examine the objects of its love." If we love justice as *justicia,* a form of right ordering, that is a love worthy of binding us together. But suppose what unites us is a love of self-interest and its magnification of the sort I submit we are in the midst of at present—caught up in a bubble defined by how well NASDAQ and the New York Stock Exchange are doing on any given day. This impoverished understanding of what binds us impoverishes us as human subjects, in turn. We can scarcely love our neighbor if we are out to make a killing at his expense. Let there be no doubt about it: There are always winners and losers. Trickle-down economics may work up to a point. But the trickle dwindles to a few drops and dries up altogether before it gets to all too many among us. The gap between the many—admittedly—who do well or better within this bubble, one that is bound to burst sooner or later, and the tens of thousands, a minority but a substantial minority, who do not is growing. And that helps to erode the delicate filaments of commonality as well: it is harder for us to see what we have in common with one another if huge gulfs divide us.

Disengagement versus Engagement

There are those within the Christian community who make powerful arguments that the task of Christians is to witness to the truth but not in a political way. They downgrade the tasks of magistracy that Augustine insists we are obliged to take up. These are seen as unworthy by contrast to the mission of offering up a pure witness to the world. The problem with such a stance is that it becomes arrogant: All the engagements with the world that take place in and through politics are construed as fit only for those with a lower or lesser calling, those with "dirty hands." As for us, so this argument too often suggests, we are above the fray, ongoingly judging it without taking up the burdens of free responsibility for this state of things in any substantial way. This can lead to what Bonhoeffer calls "cheap grace," the sort displayed by one he labels the "man of virtue" who flees from engagement with the world. Here is Bonhoeffer, mincing no words: "Here and there people flee from public altercation into the sanctuary of private *virtuousness*. But anyone who does this must shut his mouth and his eyes to the injustice around him. Only at the cost of self-deception can he keep himself pure from the contamination arising from responsible action. In spite of all that he does, what he leaves undone will rob him of his peace of mind."

An obligation that falls upon Christians as citizens is to advance a more capacious and generous understanding of both Christianity and politics than one that preaches a form of private or group virtue by contrast to the sullied majority of us on the one hand, or one that has only a narrow politics of self-interest to offer and to demand be represented in Washington, D.C., on the other. I believe we do get the kind of representation we deserve, for the most part, up to and including the shameless behavior of Bill Clinton, a president who treated the White House as a singles bar, demanding staff support in so doing. We need to think about the quality of mind and heart and spirit of those called by us to act on our behalf. Because we seem to have decided tacitly that politics is about delivering the goodies and political leadership has nothing whatsoever to do with the quality of heart, mind, and spirit of those who occupy positions of political power—so long as those bells clang happily at closing hour on Wall Street—we have acquiesced in severely restricting "the scope of political discourse."

Again, Lovin: "If politics avoids the potentially divisive question of what our humanity requires of us, it cannot discuss truth and excellence. It cannot try to persuade us to want something different from what we already want, cannot tell us that we would be better people if we did." A politics of "instrumental goods" is a politics that flees from tapping and helping to make manifest what Lincoln called "the better angels of our nature." We seem to have succeeded all too well in stifling dissent "by creating a narcissistic culture, in which people do not care what happens to their neighbors. . . ." Now, I mentioned at the outset the number of college students called to neighbor-love and service, but when asked why they are doing this they falter. It "makes me feel good," they say. I "feel better about myself." If we cannot do better than that in characterizing our own neighborly impulses, I submit that these impulses will gradually wither on the vine as the pressures of economic life overtake us once we depart the hallowed halls of ivy and enter what is sometimes called "the real world." A few final words from Lovin: "In its divided and sometimes chaotic reality, politics is the best approximation we have of a community of discourse in which our ideas about the human good could be tested against all the real human beings that the ideas are about. . . . Only when we understand politics in those terms can we avoid reducing it to an instrument by which we gain our ends at the expense of others who are less skilled in manipulating the system."

Principles of Engagement

Let us assume that we have embraced the claim on us to be salt and light to the world. We are pilgrims in "our empire." How do we try to make more generous what it means to embody our status as God's creatures, made to serve Him wittily "in the tangle of our minds"? There are some specific cultural-political tasks I would like to lift up for your consideration. I can offer only brief intimations of each of these tasks. I lay them out more fully in *Who Are We? Critical Reflections and Hopeful Possibilities.*

These principles involve responsible action and forthright engagement with the world. I am not suggesting public policies here or even hinting that there are definitive resolutions to the matters I shall put before you. These tasks involve engagement with others that will often have an edge of conflict of the sort that aims to open up debate, not shut it down; that aims to prick people's consciences and to call forth our clearest thoughts rather than to shut down our moral instincts and drive us into nostrums and ideology.

First, those poised delicately between *contra mundum* and *amor mundi* must insist that we name things accurately and appropriately. This is vital because one extraordinary sign of our times is a process of radical alteration in language, understanding, and meaning. We are painfully aware of what happens when totalitarian regimes have the power to control language and to cover mass murder with the rhetoric of improvement of the race or ridding a nation of vicious class enemies. Even mercy and compassion get dragged into it, if one recalls the National Socialist regime's effort to rid Germany of persons with disabilities and inherited diseases or ailments. But we are much less attuned to distortion in our own language. Think, for example, of the language employed by the so-called "right to die" effort, one that deploys the dominant terms of our culture's discourse—compassion (let's end suffering now) and rights. The notorious Dr. Kevorkian, in common with a good many others, rails against those who refuse to take on board his insistence that people should have a "right" to kill themselves and to have medical assistance in doing so, whenever they see fit. Kevorkian's philosophy is the crudest utilitarianism imaginable. Indeed, he sees assisted suicide and euthanasia as stalking horses "for a wider social vision of routine experimentation upon dying people and walk-in municipal suicide centres where the ill and merely disgruntled will be helped at public expense to shuffle off this mortal coil. These will be manned by salaried specialists in death called obitriatists who practice patholysis, the dissolution of all suffering," this according to a detailed report from the *Independent* of London. He also argues for experimentation on the bodies of prisoners condemned to execution—they are going to die anyway, so why not? Once in a while we really are on a slippery slope. If we have embraced the view that we are all alone with our "rights"—having denied relational personhood—why should we be queasy about exercising that "right" alone at the end, in a van parked in a parking lot somewhere with the bodies that are the end product being dumped on the doorsteps of hospitals or left for the police to find. There are many ways to ill-dignify the bodies of the ill and dying and this is surely one. Yet, as a culture, we seem to have ceded the high ground to those who use the language of rights and compassion to these distorted ends. Let's take back the language! This is a civic task of the most exigent importance. Let's think of more effective ways to minister to the bodies of the dying and to remind our fellow citizens that rights are not possessions of utterly alone selves but are intrinsically relational. Politics must not be permitted to succumb to such crassly utilitarian horrors.

Second, those engaging the world from a Christian stance must ongoingly witness to incarnational being-in-the-world. We are called to cultivate citizens who make visible before the world the fullness, dignity, and wonder of creation in the midst of its wanton destruction. This sounds mysterious but it isn't. Modern deadness is all around us—the conviction that the world is so much matter to manipulate, that abstract signs and symbols entirely of our own creation that can be sent whirring 'round the globe in milliseconds are the reality that counts, and that individuation as a kind of radical aloneness simply is the human condition. The incarnational moment reasserts itself as part of what the Pontifical Academy for Life calls an "authentic culture of life, which should . . . accept the reality of the finiteness and natural limits of earthly life. Only in this way can death not be reduced to a merely clinical event or be deprived of its personal and social dimension." I submit that in the depths of our being, we know this. It is an awareness that our culture is clouding over but it reappears as phantoms and hauntings. We know that people deserve dignified treatment as a constitutive feature of life's pilgrimage. We know that everyone is someone's mother, father, son, daughter, wife, husband, child, grandparent, friend, those by whom we should be accompanied as we move through life toward death within a surround that speaks to our dignity as persons. This we cannot allow a culture—our culture—to forget.

Finally, citizens who are Christian and called, therefore, to witness and to live in hope must assure that their churches play a critical role as interpreters of the culture to the culture. There are few such interpretive public sites available in this era of media saturation. Now, you cannot engage the culture if, in common with too many contemporary culture critics, you loathe and despise it, or have given up hope for it entirely. If at one point in our culture, this denunciatory tack was the purview of the political left with its hatred of all things "Amerikan"—spelled with a "k"—now such voices are more frequently heard coming from right of center. America is construed as one seething fleshpot ready to implode. But if the culture were really beyond redemption, it would cast doubts on creation itself and its goodness; surely, that cannot be bleached out entirely. Think here of the horror of the Columbine High School massacre and the shocked lamentations that succeeded it—proof positive, to some, that young people were going to hell. Two young men were in hell, that's for sure, captured by the darkness and representations of evil and they struck out, apparently targeting explicitly students who voiced their belief in God. Some of those wounded and killed were shot because they were carrying Bibles or said they believed in God, at least so many eye- and ear-witnesses—and survivors—tell us. Who can imagine such courage under such terrible circumstances? Recall as well what so many students did during the course of the massacre and after: At risk to their own lives, they ushered frantic and paralyzed classmates to safety; this is how one young man died. They struggled to keep their coach and teacher, Dave Sanders, alive, stanching his wounds with their torn T-shirts, fashioning a stretcher from table legs, and when it was clear he was bleeding to death they held him and prayed with and for him and showed him pictures of his family. They loved and cared for one another. In the aftermath, they put up signs and crosses and offered prayers and devout promises to help rebuild a community that would constitute a living memorial to their classmates who had perished.

This is, to put it bluntly, a hell of a thing for kids to go through. But the way in which these young people went through it should help us to savor living hope rather than to dwell exclusively on the violence and to lament all things adolescent. It should also forestall a triumphalist tone from churches and the Christian community, for that is not the sort of engagement that actually engages; it leads our fellow citizens, as troubled and perplexed as we are, to flee in the opposite direction.

Do we seem to be very far way indeed from Washington, D.C. Yes and no. If civic life is about how we order a way of life in common together, the cultural moments I have noted are at the heart of the matter, not at the periphery. What can D.C. do or not do? There are many things we could forebear from doing—I mentioned questions of economic and tax policy at the beginning—that now virtually guarantee that people are drawn away from their families and communities. There are many things we could do and that require cultural and civic initiatives and government action, including regulation of virtually unregulated industries. Why is it "censorship" to build-in incentives and disincentives to turn the media giants away from their absorption with violence and throw-away relationships and sex are disconnected from any notion of respect for the bodies of others? Surely as a culture we can find ways of altering the framework and the surround that presses in on us all but most heavily on overburdened parents and teachers, those charged most directly with the tasks of formation.

I hope I have said enough to convince you that although you might not be interested in politics, it is very interested in you. How do you respond? Through a flight into that virtuousness Bonhoeffer called spurious? Or through faithful engagement at the risk of dirtying one's hands a bit with the messy task of caring for the world into which you have been born and from which you cannot flee? Christians, above all, should find ways to love, to cherish, and to correct the civic world.

Chapter Six

Reason, Freedom, and the Rule of Law

THE POLITICAL SIGNIFICANCE OF
MAN'S SPIRITUAL POWERS

Robert P. George

The idea of law and the ideal of the rule of law are central to the natural law, and more generally the Western, tradition of thought about public or "political" order.[1] St. Thomas Aquinas went so far as to declare that "it belongs to the very notion of a people [ad rationem populi] that the people's dealings with each other be regulated by just precepts of law."[2] In our own time, Pope John Paul II has forcefully reaffirmed the status of the rule of law as a requirement of fundamental political justice.[3] For all the romantic appeal of "palm tree justice" or "Solomonic judging," and despite the sometimes decidedly unromantic qualities of living by preordained legal rules, the natural law tradition affirms that justice itself requires that people be governed in accordance with the principles of legality.

Among the core concerns of natural law theorists and other legal philosophers in the second half of the twentieth century have been the meaning, content, and moral significance of the rule of law. The renewal of interest in this ancient question, or set of questions, has had to do above all, I think, with the unprecedented rise and fall of totalitarian regimes. In the aftermath of the defeat of Nazism, legal philosophers of every religious persuasion tested their legal theories by asking, for example, whether the

ROBERT P. GEORGE, McCormick Professor of Jurisprudence, Princeton University, and Director of the James Madison Program in American Ideals and Institutions, has authored *Making Men Moral: Civil Liberties and Public Morality*, *In Defense of Natural Law*, and *The Clash of Orthodoxies: Law, Religion, and Morality in Crisis*.

Nazi regime constituted a *legal* system in any meaningful sense. In the wake of communism's collapse in Europe, legal scholars and others are urgently trying to understand the role of legal procedures and institutions in creating and sustaining decent democratic regimes. It has been in this particular context that Pope John Paul II has had occasion to stress the moral importance of the rule of law.

Lon L. Fuller and the Rule of Law

One of the signal achievements of legal philosophy in the twentieth century was Lon L. Fuller's explication of the content of the rule of law.[4] Reflecting on law as a "purposive" enterprise—the subjecting of human behavior to the governance of rules—Fuller identified eight constitutive elements of legality. These are (1) the prospectivity (i.e., non-retroactivity) of legal rules, (2) the absence of impediments to compliance with the rules by those subject to them, (3) the promulgation of the rules, (4) their clarity, (5) their coherence with one another, (6) their constancy over time, (7) their generality of application, and (8) the congruence between official action and declared rule. Irrespective of whether a legal system or a body of law is good or bad—that is to say, substantively just or unjust—*to the extent* that it truly is a legal system or a body of law it will, to some significant degree, exemplify these elements.

It was a mark of Fuller's sophistication, I think, that he noticed that the rule of law is a *matter of degree.* Its constitutive elements are exemplified *to a greater or lesser extent* by actual legal systems or bodies of law. Legal systems exemplify the rule of law *to the extent that* the rules constituting them are prospective, susceptible of being complied with, promulgated, clear, and so forth.

FULLER'S CRITICS

Even Fuller's critics recognized his achievement in explicating the content of the rule of law. What they objected to was Fuller's claims—or, in any event, what they took to be Fuller's claims—on its behalf. Provocatively, Fuller asserted that, taken together, the elements of the rule of law, though in themselves procedural, nevertheless constitute what he called an "internal morality of law" (hence the title of Fuller's major work on the subject of the rule of law, *The Morality of Law*). Moreover, he explicitly presented his account of the rule of law as a challenge to the dominant "legal positivism" of his time. According to Fuller, once we recognize that law, precisely as such, *has* an internal morality, it becomes clear that the "conceptual separation of law and morality" which forms the core of the "positivist" understanding of law, legal obligation and the practical functioning of legal institutions cannot be maintained.

These claims drew sharp criticism from, among others, Herbert Hart, the Oxford legal philosopher whose magisterial 1961 book *The Concept of Law*[5] both substantially revised and dramatically revitalized the positivist tradition in analytical jurisprudence. In a now famous review essay in the *Harvard Law Review,* Hart accused Fuller of, in effect, engaging in a semantic sleight of hand.[6] According to Hart, there isn't the slightest reason to suppose that the constitutive elements of legality which Fuller correctly and very usefully identified should be accounted as a "morality" of any sort. As Fuller himself seemed to concede, unjust, or otherwise morally bad, law can exemplify the procedural elements of legality just as fully as just law can. But if that is true, then it is worse than merely tendentious to claim that these elements constitute an "internal *morality* of law."

Indeed, Fuller's critics have observed that even the most wicked rulers sometimes have purely self-interested reasons to put into place, and operate strictly in accordance with, legal procedures. Yet even the strictest adherence to the forms of legality cannot ensure that the laws they enact and enforce will be substantively just or even minimally decent. Replying to Hart and other critics, Fuller argued that the historical record shows that thoroughly evil regimes, such as the Nazi regime, consistently fail to observe even the formal principles of legality. In practice the Nazis, to stay with the example, freely departed from the rule of law whenever it suited their purposes to do so. So Fuller defied Hart to provide "significant examples of regimes that have combined a faithful adherence to the [rule of law] with a brutal indifference to justice and human welfare."[7]

Now, it is important to see that Fuller's claim here is not that regimes can never perpetrate injustices—even grave injustices—while respecting the elements of the rule of law. It is the weaker, yet by no means trivial, claim that those regimes which respect the rule of law do not, and cannot so long as they adhere to the rule of law, degenerate into truly monstrous tyrannies like the Nazis.

Still, Fuller's critics were unpersuaded. My own esteemed teacher, Joseph Raz, one of Hart's greatest students and now his literary executor, pursued a more radical line of argument to deflate Fuller's claim that the elements of the rule of law constitute an internal morality. Raz suggested that the rule of law is a purely instrumental, rather than any sort of *moral,* good. He analogized the rule of law to a sharp knife—an *efficient* instrument, and in that non-moral sense "good," but equally serviceable in morally good and *bad* causes.[8] Indeed, according to Raz, insofar as the institution and maintenance of legal procedures improve governmental efficiency, they increase the potential for evildoing of wicked rulers.

FULLER'S CONVERTS

Fuller's arguments have, however, won some converts. Most notably, perhaps, Neil MacCormick, who had once shared Raz's view that the requirements of the rule of law "can in principle be as well-observed by those whose laws wreak great substantive injustice as by those whose laws are in substance as just as they can possibly be," eventually revised his opinion to give some credit to Fuller's claim that the elements of the rule of law constitute a kind of internal morality:

> There is always something to be said for treating people with formal fairness, that is, in a rational and predictable way, setting public standards for citizens' conduct and officials' responses thereto, standards with which one can judge compliance or non-compliance, rather than leaving everything to discretionary and potentially arbitrary decision. That indeed is what we mean by the "Rule of Law." Where it is observed, people are confronted by a state which treats them as *rational agents due some respect as such.* It applies fairly whatever standards of conduct and of judgment it applies. This has real value, and independent value, even where the substance of what is done falls short of any relevant ideal of substantive justice.[9]

MacCormick's revised understanding strikes me as sounder than the contrary understanding of Hart and Raz, who refuse to accord to the requirements of the rule of law any of the sort of more-than-merely-instrumental value that MacCormick labels "independent." Plainly it is the case that well-intentioned rulers who genuinely care for justice and the common good of the communities they govern will strive for procedural fairness—and will do so, in part, because they understand that people, as rational agents, are due the respect that is paid them when officials eschew arbitrary decision-making and operate according to law. And we can understand this without the need for sociological inquiry into the way things are done by officials in more or less just regimes. Rather, it is the fruit of reflection on what such officials *ought* to do because they *owe* it to those under their governance. But if I am right about this, then respect for the requirements of the rule of law *is not a morally neutral matter*—despite the fact that the elements of the rule of law are themselves procedural. Rather, rulers or officials have *moral reasons* and, inasmuch as these reasons are generally conclusive, a *moral obligation* to respect the requirements of the rule of law.

The Moral Obligations of Rulers

Of course, respect for the rule of law does not exhaust the moral obligations of rulers or officials toward those subject to their governance. Nor, as Fuller's critics such as Hart and Raz correctly observe, does respect for the rule of law guarantee that the substance of the laws will be just. If Raz went too far in one direction by treating the rule of law as a morally neutral "efficient instrument," proponents of the rule of law can easily go too far in the other direction by supposing that the achievement and maintenance of the rule of law immunizes a regime against grave injustice and even tyranny.

Here historical and sociological inquiry is the antidote to overblown claims. Apartheid and even slavery have coexisted with the rule of law. And those legal positivists who claimed that even the Nazi regime worked much of its evil through formally lawful means were not without evidence to support their view. When it comes to the question of the alleged incompatibility of respect for the rule of law with grave substantive injustice, I would venture on behalf of the rule of law only the following modest thesis: An unjust regime's adherence to the procedural requirements of legality, so long as it lasts, has the virtue of limiting the rulers' freedom of maneuver in ways that will generally reduce, to some extent at least, their capacity for evildoing. Potential victims of injustice at the hands of wicked rulers will generally benefit, if only to a limited extent, from their rulers' willingness, whatever its motivation, to respect the requirements of the rule of law.

Philosophers of law in the natural law tradition from Plato to John Finnis have warned that wherever the rule of law enjoys prestige, ill-intentioned rulers will find it expedient to—and will—adhere to constitutional procedures and other legal forms as a means of maintaining or enhancing their political power.[10] Plato himself had no illusions that adherence to such procedures and forms would *guarantee* substantively just rule. Nevertheless, he noticed that even apart from the self-interested motives of evil rulers to act sometimes in accordance with principles of legality, decent rulers always and everywhere have reason to respect these principles, for procedural fairness is itself a requirement of substantive justice—one that is always desirable in human relations and, in particular, in the relationships between those exercising political power and those over whom such power is exercised.

Where the rule of law is respected, there obtains between the rulers and the ruled a certain reciprocity. Now, this reciprocity will surely be useful in securing certain desirable ends to which it is a means. I have in mind, for example, various elements of social order, including efficiency in the regulation and/or delivery of public services, and political stability, particularly in times of stress. But Plato's point, and I see no reason to doubt it, is the moral-philosophical one that, given the dignity of human beings, this sort of reciprocity is more than *merely* a means to other ends. As such, it ought to be protected and advanced wherever possible, and it may not be sacrificed lightly even for the sake of other important goods.

Now, there is a lot packed into my little phrase—more Kantian in flavor, I suppose, than Platonic—"given the dignity of human beings." Although most people have moral objections to cruelty toward animals, we do not consider that pets or farm animals are to be governed in accordance with the requirements of the rule of law. Within the bounds of decency, we hope, the farmer resorts rather to Pavlovian methods, or, indeed, to whatever it takes to get the chickens to lay and the cows into pasture. Indeed, it would be pointless to attempt to rule nonhuman animals by law since laws cannot function for chickens and cows as *reasons* for their actions. The farmer, rather, causes or at least attempts to cause the animal behavior he desires. Humans, by contrast, can be governed by law because legal rules can function in people's practical deliberation as what Herbert Hart described—in an important break with his positivist predecessors, Bentham and Austin, who conceived of legal rules as *causes* of human behavior, rather than as *reasons*—as "content-independent, peremptory reasons for action."[11]

Rationality and the Rule of Law

Virtually all philosophical accounts of human dignity stress the moral significance of human rationality. People are indeed, as Neil MacCormick says, "due some respect, as rational agents." But if this is true, as I believe it is, then perhaps it is worth pausing to consider why and how governance in accordance with the requirements of the rule of law treats people with some of the respect that they are due as *rational* agents. What is it about human rationality that entails a dignity which is violated when rulers treat those subject to their rule the way farmers treat livestock?

Today, when one speaks of human rationality in virtually any context one will be understood to be referring to what Aristotle labeled "theoretical" rationality. Theoretical, as opposed to what Aristotle labeled "practical," rationality inquires into *what is, was, or could be the case* about the natural, social, or supernatural world; practical rationality identifies possibilities for choice and action and inquires into *what ought to be done. Merely* theoretically rational beings, however, could not be ruled by law and would, in any event, no more deserve to be ruled by law than computers deserve such rule. It is hard to see how even theoretically rational agents who, *unlike computers,* (1) experienced feelings of desire and (2) brought intellectual operations to bear in efficiently satisfying their desires could be due the respect implied by the rule of law or other requirements of morality. This is why instrumentalist theories of practical reason such as Hobbes's[12] or Hume's[13]—not to mention the various contemporary reductionist accounts of human behavior which understand human beings as computers who are motivated by desires—have difficulty providing an even remotely plausible account of human dignity, and only rarely offer to do so. Such agents would not be capable of exercising *practical* reason and making *moral* choices. Their behavior could only be caused, ultimately either by external coercion or internal compulsion.[14] Lacking the capacity ultimately to understand and act on the basis of more-than-merely-instrumental *reasons,* they would literally be beyond freedom and dignity.

My proposition is that the rationality which entitles people to the sort of respect exemplified in the principles of the rule of law is not primarily the rationality that enables people to solve mathematical problems, or understand the human neural system, or develop cures for diseases, or inquire into the origins of the universe or even the existence and attributes of God. It is, rather, the rationality that enables us to judge that mathematical problems are to be solved, that the neural system is to be understood, that diseases are to be cured, and that God is to be known and loved. It is, moreover, the capacity to distinguish fully reasonable possibilities for choice and action from possibilities that, while rationally grounded, fall short of all that reason demands.[15]

In short, the dignity that calls forth the respect due to rational agents in the form of, among other things, governance in accordance with the rule of law flows from our nature as *practically* intelligent beings, that is, beings whose nature is to understand and act on more-than-merely-instrumental reasons. The capacity to understand and act on such reasons stands in a relationship of mutual entailment with the human capacity for free choice, that is, our capacity to *deliberate and choose* between or among open possibilities, i.e., options, that are provided by "basic human goods," i.e., more-than-merely-instrumental reasons.

Free Choice and the Rule of Law

Free choice *exists* just insofar as people have, are aware of, and can act upon such reasons; people have, are aware of, and can act upon such reasons just insofar as they have free choice. But if it is true that people possess reason and freedom, then they enjoy what can only be described as *spiritual* powers,[16] and, it might even be said, a certain sharing in divine power–viz., the power to bring into being that which one reasonably judges to be worth bringing into being (something "of value"), but which one is in no sense compelled or "caused" to bring into being.

What is God-like, albeit, of course, in a very limited way, is the human power to be an "uncaused causing." This, I believe, is the central meaning and significance of the otherwise extraordinarily puzzling biblical teaching that man unlike other creatures is made in the very "image and likeness of God."[17] This teaching expresses in theological terms, and proposes as a matter of revealed truth, the philosophical proposition I have been advancing about the dignity flowing from the nature of human beings as *practically* intelligent creatures. Its upshot is not that human beings may not legitimately be ruled, but that they must be ruled in ways that accord them the respect they are due "as rational agents." Among other things, it requires that the rule to which human beings are subjected is the *rule of law*.

Reflection on the relationship of human reason and freedom—and the theological significance of this relationship in a tradition crucially shaped by the biblical account of man as a possessor of spiritual powers and, indeed, as an *imago dei*—helps, I believe, to make sense of the centrality of law, and the rule of law, in Western thought about political morality. In particular, it helps to explain the stress laid upon the ideal of the rule of law as a fundamental principle of political justice in the strand of the tradition stretching from early and medieval Christian thinkers to John Paul II.

Notes

1. The idea of law and the ideal of the rule of law have always been central to the political thought of Christian philosophers and theologians. This idea and ideal were by no means Christian inventions, however. They were articulated and developed in pre-Christian classical and Jewish traditions of thought. The treatment of the subject in the writings of St. Thomas Aquinas is, unsurprisingly, indebted to Plato and especially Aristotle, as well as to the Hebrew Bible.

2. St. Thomas Aquinas, *Summa Theologiae,* I–II, q. 105, a. 2c.

3. See the encyclical letter of Pope John Paul II, *Solicitudo Rei Socialis* (1987).

4. See especially Lon L. Fuller, *The Morality of Law* (New Haven, Conn.: Yale University Press, 1964).

5. H. L. A. Hart, *The Concept of Law* (Oxford: Clarendon Press, 1961).

6. H. L. A. Hart, "Review of Lon L. Fuller, *The Morality of Law,*" *Harvard Law Review* 78 (1965): 1281.

7. Fuller, *The Morality of Law,* 2nd ed., with "Reply to Critics" (1969), 154.

8. See Joseph Raz, "The Rule of Law and Its Virtue," *Law Quarterly Review* 93 (1977): 208.

9. Neil MacCormick, "Natural Law and the Separation of Law and Morals," in Robert P. George, ed., *Natural Law Theory: Contemporary Essays* (Oxford: Clarendon Press, 1992), 105–33, 123 (emphasis supplied).

10. See Plato, *Statesman,* 291a–303d, John Finnis, *Natural Law and Natural Rights* (Oxford: Clarendon Press, 1980), 274.

11. See H. L. A. Hart, *Essays on Bentham* (Oxford: Clarendon Press, 1983), ch. 10. For a particularly illuminating account of the differences between reasons and causes, see Daniel N. Robinson, *Philosophy of Psychology* (New York: Columbia University Press, 1985), 50–57.

12. See Thomas Hobbes, *Leviathan* (1651), pt. 1, ch. 8.

13. See David Hume, *A Treatise of Human Nature* (1740), bk. 2, pt. 3, sec. III.

14. See Germain Grisez, Joseph M. Boyle, Jr., and Olaf Tollefsen, *Free Choice: A Self-Referential Argument* (Notre Dame, Ind.: University of Notre Dame Press, 1976).

15. For an explanation of this point, see Robert P. George, "Natural Law Ethics," in Philip L. Quinn and Charles Taliaferro, eds., *A Companion to Philosophy of Religion*

(Oxford: Blackwell Publishers, Ltd., 1997), ch. 58. See also Robert P. George, *Making Men Moral: Civil Liberties and Public Morality* (Oxford: Clarendon Press, 1993), 8–18.

16. On the status of free choices as "spiritual" entities, see Germain Grisez, *The Way of the Lord Jesus, Vol. 1: Christian Moral Principles* (Chicago: Franciscan Herald Press, 1983), 50–52.

17. "[M]an is said to be made in God's image, insofar as the image implies *an intelligent being endowed with free-will and self-movement:* now that we have treated of the exemplar, i.e., God, and those things which come forth from the power of God in accordance with his will; it remains for us to treat of His image, i.e., man, inasmuch as he too is the principle of his actions, as having free will and control of his actions." St. Thomas Aquinas, *Summa Theologiae,* I–II, Prologue (emphasis in the original).

Chapter Seven

Darwin's Black Box

Michael J. Behe

A Series of Eyes

How do we see? In the nineteenth century the anatomy of the eye was known in great detail and its sophisticated features astounded everyone who was familiar with them. Scientists of the time correctly observed that if a person were so unfortunate as to be missing one of the eye's many integrated features, such as the lens, or iris, or ocular muscles, the inevitable result would be a severe loss of vision or outright blindness. So it was concluded that the eye could only function if it were nearly intact.

Charles Darwin knew about the eye too. In *The Origin of Species* Darwin dealt with many objections to his theory of evolution by natural selection. He discussed the problem of the eye in a section of the book appropriately entitled "Organs of extreme perfection and complication." Somehow, for evolution to be believable, Darwin had to convince the public that complex organs could be formed gradually, in a step-by-step process.

He succeeded brilliantly. Cleverly, Darwin didn't try to discover a real pathway that evolution might have used to make the eye. Instead, he pointed to modern animals with different kinds of eyes, ranging from the simple to the complex, and suggested that the evolution of the human eye might have involved similar organs as intermediates.

MICHAEL J. BEHE, Professor of Biological Sciences at Lehigh University, wrote *Darwin's Black Box: The Biochemical Challenge to Evolution,* which has been reviewed in more than 100 periodicals, including the *New York Times, Nature, Philosophy of Science,* and *Christianity Today.*

Here is a paraphrase of Darwin's argument. Although humans have complex camera-type eyes, many animals get by with less. Some tiny creatures have just a simple group of pigmented cells—not much more than a light-sensitive spot. That simple arrangement can hardly be said to confer vision, but it can sense light and dark, and so it meets the creature's needs. The light-sensing organ of some starfishes is somewhat more sophisticated. Their eye is located in a depressed region. This allows the animal to sense which direction the light is coming from, since the curvature of the depression blocks off light from some directions. If the curvature becomes more pronounced, the directional sense of the eye improves. But more curvature lessens the amount of light that enters the eye, decreasing its sensitivity. The sensitivity can be increased by placement of gelatinous material in the cavity to act as a lens. Some modern animals have eyes with such crude lenses. Gradual improvements in the lens could then provide an image of increasing sharpness, as the requirements of the animal's environment dictated.

Using reasoning like this, Darwin convinced many of his readers that an evolutionary pathway leads from the simplest light-sensitive spot to the sophisticated camera-eye of man. But the question remains, how did vision begin? Darwin persuaded much of the world that a modern eye evolved gradually from a simpler structure, but he did not even try to explain where his starting point—the "simple" light-sensitive spot—came from. On the contrary, Darwin dismissed the question of the eye's ultimate origin:

> How a nerve comes to be sensitive to light hardly concerns us more than how life itself originated.[1]

He had an excellent reason for declining the question: It was completely beyond nineteenth-century science. How the eye works—that is, what happens when a photon of light first hits the retina—simply could not be answered at that time. As a matter of fact, no question about the underlying mechanisms of life could be answered. How did animal muscles cause movement? How did photosynthesis work? How was energy extracted from food? How did the body fight infection? No one knew.

To Darwin vision was a black box but today, after the hard, cumulative work of many biochemists, we are approaching answers to the question of sight. To get a flavor of what a theory of evolution must explain let's take

Darwin's example of the eye and examine a few of the molecular details of vision that have been discovered by modern science. When light first strikes the retina a photon interacts with a molecule called 11-cis-retinal, which rearranges within picoseconds to trans-retinal. The change in the shape of retinal forces a change in the shape of the protein, rhodopsin, to which the retinal is tightly bound. The protein's metamorphosis alters its behavior, making it stick to another protein called transducin. Before bumping into activated rhodopsin, transducin had tightly bound a small molecule called GDP. But when transducin interacts with activated rhodopsin, the GDP falls off and a molecule called GTP binds to transducin. (GTP is closely related to, but critically different from, GDP.)

GTP-transducin-activated rhodopsin now binds to a protein called phosphodiesterase, located in the inner membrane of the cell. When attached to activated rhodopsin and its entourage, the phosphodiesterase acquires the ability to chemically cut a molecule called cGMP (a chemical relative of both GDP and GTP). Initially there are a lot of cGMP molecules in the cell, but the phosphodiesterase lowers its concentration, like a pulled plug lowers the water level in a bathtub.

Another membrane protein that binds cGMP is called an ion channel. It acts as a gateway that regulates the number of sodium ions in the cell. Normally the ion channel allows sodium ions to flow into the cell, while a separate protein actively pumps them out again. The dual action of the ion channel and pump keeps the level of sodium ions in the cell within a narrow range. When the amount of cGMP is reduced because of cleavage by the phosphodiesterase, the ion channel closes, causing the cellular concentration of positively charged sodium ions to be reduced. This causes an imbalance of charge across the cell membrane which, finally, causes a current to be transmitted down the optic nerve to the brain. The result, when interpreted by the brain, is vision.

This description is just a sketchy overview of the biochemistry of vision. Ultimately, though, this is what it means to "explain" vision. This is the level of explanation for which biological science must aim. In order to truly understand a function, one must understand in detail every relevant step in the process. The relevant steps in biological processes occur ultimately at the molecular level, so a satisfactory explanation of a biological phenomenon—such as vision, or digestion or immunity—must include its molecular explanation.

Now that the black box of vision has been opened it is no longer enough for an "evolutionary explanation" of that power to consider only the anatomical structures of whole eyes, as Darwin did in the nineteenth century and as popularizers of evolution continue to do today. Each of the anatomical steps and structures Darwin thought were so simple actually involves staggeringly complicated biochemical processes that cannot be papered over with rhetoric. The details of life are handled by molecular machines. Darwin's theory will stand or fall on its ability to explain them.

Irreducible Complexity

So how can we decide if Darwin's theory can account for the complexity of molecular life? It turns out that Darwin himself set a standard. He acknowledged that:

> If it could be demonstrated that any complex organ existed which could not possibly have been formed by numerous, successive, slight modifications, my theory would absolutely break down.[2]

But what type of biological system could not be formed by "numerous, successive, slight modifications"?

Well, for starters, a system that is irreducibly complex. Irreducible complexity is just a fancy phrase I use to mean a single system which is composed of several interacting parts, and where the removal of any one of the parts causes the system to cease functioning.

Let's consider an everyday example of irreducible complexity: the humble mousetrap. The mousetraps that my family uses consist of a number of parts. There are (1) a flat wooden platform to act as a base; (2) a metal hammer, which does the actual job of crushing the little mouse; (3) a spring with extended ends to press against the platform and the hammer when the trap is charged; (4) a sensitive catch which releases when slight pressure is applied; and (5) a metal bar which connects to the catch and holds the hammer back when the trap is charged. Now you can't catch a mouse with just a platform, add a spring and catch a few more mice, add a holding bar and catch a few more. All the pieces of the mousetrap have to be in place before you catch any mice. Therefore the mousetrap is irreducibly complex.

An irreducibly complex system cannot be produced directly by numerous, successive, slight modifications of a precursor system, because any precursor to an irreducibly complex system that is missing a part is by definition nonfunctional. An irreducibly complex biological system, if there is such a thing, would be a powerful challenge to Darwinian evolution. Since natural selection can only choose systems that are already working, then if a biological system cannot be produced gradually it would have to arise as an integrated unit for natural selection to have anything to act on.

Let me add a word of caution. Demonstration that a system is irreducibly complex is not a proof that there is absolutely no gradual route to its production. Although an irreducibly complex system can't be produced directly, one can't definitively rule out the possibility of an indirect, circuitous route. However, as the complexity of an interacting system increases, the likelihood of such an indirect route drops precipitously. And as the number of unexplained, irreducibly complex biological systems increases, our confidence that Darwin's criterion of failure has been met skyrockets toward the maximum that science allows.

The Cilium

Now, mousetraps are one thing, biochemical systems are another. So we must ask, are any biochemical systems irreducibly complex? Yes, it turns out that many are. A good example is the cilium. Cilia are hairlike structures on the surfaces of many animal and lower plant cells that can move fluid over the cell's surface or "row" single cells through a fluid. In humans, for example, cells lining the respiratory tract each have about 200 cilia that beat in synchrony to sweep mucus towards the throat for elimination. What is the structure of a cilium? A cilium consists of a bundle of fibers called an axoneme. An axoneme contains a ring of nine double "microtubules" surrounding two central single microtubules. Each outer doublet consists of a ring of thirteen filaments (subfiber A) fused to an assembly of ten filaments (subfiber B). The filaments of the microtubules are composed of two proteins called alpha and beta tubulin. The eleven microtubules forming an axoneme are held together by three types of connectors: subfibers A are joined to the central microtubules by radial spokes; adjacent outer doublets are joined by linkers of a highly elastic protein called nexin; and the central microtubules are joined by a connecting bridge. Finally, every subfiber A bears two arms, an inner arm and an outer arm, both containing a protein called dynein.

Although even this seems complex, a brief description can't do justice to the full complexity of the cilium, which has been shown by biochemical analysis to contain about 200 separate kinds of protein parts.

But how does a cilium work? Experiments have shown that ciliary motion results from the chemically powered "walking" of the dynein arms on one microtubule up a second microtubule so that the two microtubules slide past each other. The protein cross-links between microtubules in a cilium prevent neighboring microtubules from sliding past each other by more than a short distance. These cross-links, therefore, convert the dynein-induced sliding motion to a bending motion of the entire axoneme.

Now, let us consider what this implies. What components are needed for a cilium to work? Ciliary motion certainly requires microtubules; otherwise, there would be no strands to slide. Additionally we require a motor, or else the microtubules of the cilium would lie stiff and motionless. Furthermore, we require linkers to tug on neighboring strands, converting the sliding motion into a bending motion and preventing the structure from falling apart. All of these parts are required to perform one function: ciliary motion. Just as a mousetrap does not work unless all of its constituent parts are present, ciliary motion simply does not exist in the absence of microtubules, connectors, and motors. Therefore, we can conclude that the cilium is irreducibly complex—an enormous monkey wrench thrown into its presumed gradual Darwinian evolution.

Detection of Design

So far my criticisms of evolution are not much different from what a number of other scientists have offered. The shortcomings of Darwinian explanations have been noted by Stuart Kauffman, Lynn Margulis, Brian Goodwin, James Shapiro, and others. Where I differ from the other critics, however, is in the conclusion I draw from the complexity of cellular systems. I argue that the systems show strong evidence of design—purposeful, intentional design by an intelligent agent. I think it is safe to say that it is the conclusion of design, much more than my criticism of Darwinism, that has attracted attention. So let's look at the idea of design.

What is "design"? Design is simply the purposeful arrangement of parts. With such a broad definition it is easy to see that anything might have been designed. The coats on a rack in a restaurant may have been arranged just so by the owner before you came in. The trash and tin cans along the edge of a highway may have been placed by an artist trying to make some obscure environmental statement. On the campus of my university there are sculptures which, if I saw them lying beside the road, I would guess were the result of chance blows to a piece of scrap metal, but they were designed.

The upshot of this conclusion—that anything could have been purposely arranged—is that we can never positively rule out design. Nonetheless, it is a good rule of thumb to assume there is no design unless one can detect it. The scientific problem then becomes, how do we confidently detect design? When is it reasonable to conclude, in the absence of firsthand knowledge or eyewitness accounts, that something has been designed?

There are several ways to detect design. However, for discrete physical systems design is most easily apprehended when a number of separate, interacting components are ordered in such a way as to accomplish a function beyond the individual components. To illustrate, consider a *Far Side* cartoon by Gary Larson in which an exploring team is going through a jungle, and the lead explorer has been strung up and skewered. A companion turns to another and confides, "That's why I never walk in front." Now every person who sees the cartoon immediately knows that the trap was designed. In fact, Larson's humor depends on you recognizing the design. It wouldn't be terribly funny if the first explorer had just fallen off a cliff or a rotted tree accidentally fell on him. No, his fate was intended. But how do you know that? How does the audience apprehend that this trap was designed? You can tell that the trap was designed because of the way the parts interact with great specificity to perform a function. Like the mousetrap we saw in the beginning of the talk, no one would mistake the cartoon system for an accidental arrangement of parts. Further, all of the parts of the trap are natural components: a vine, a tree, some pieces of wood. There are no artificial, manufactured pieces. Therefore, we can come to a conclusion of design for a system composed entirely of natural parts.

Let's ask a few more questions about the *Far Side* situation. When was the trap made? Just from looking at it, you can't tell if the trap was put together an hour ago, last week, or last year, although by gathering further evidence you might be able to narrow down that question (for instance, by noting that twenty years ago the tree would not have been tall enough to support the trap). The point I wish to make here is that we apprehend design independently of knowing when the design took place. As a matter of fact, we must first recognize that there has been a design event before we can even entertain the question of when the event took place.

Who made the trap? We might guess that perhaps a resident of the jungle constructed it to defend his homeland. However, suppose over a bottle of wine later in the evening one of the other explorers confesses that he made the trap, stealing away from camp one night last month and constructing it along a path that he knew the group would later be taking. Just by looking at the trap, you can't tell who made it. Either of these possibilities is consistent with the appearance of the trap. The identity of the designer is a separate question which doesn't even arise until we apprehend that a system was designed.

Let's push this thought a little further. Where is the trap? We see it's in a jungle somewhere, but where? Suppose we were told that these folks are actually space explorers, and that they are the first people ever to land on an alien planet, light years from earth. They are exploring an alien jungle when the unfortunate lead explorer is skewered. Now, who designed the trap? Was it a member of the space party? Was it an intelligent alien? Although we can tell that the trap was designed, we cannot determine the designer's identity simply by looking at the trap. The conclusion I wish to draw here is that we can apprehend design without knowing who the designer is.

With these preliminary questions cleared out of the way I suggest that many biochemical systems were designed by an intelligent agent. Our ability to be confident of the design of the cilium or intracellular transport rests on the same principles as our ability to be confident of the design of the jungle trap: the ordering of separate components to achieve an identifiable function that depends sharply on the components.

Who did the designing, when, where, and how remain open questions that may or may not be accessible to science. But the fact of design itself can be deduced from the structure of the systems which biochemists have elucidated in the past decades.

The Battle of the Mousetrap

Since *Darwin's Black Box* (in which I further explain my views) was published, a number of criticisms have been voiced by Darwinists. I have responded to such criticisms in various forums. Here I want to focus on just one criticism—a counterexample that attacks the logic of irreducible complexity. As I will show, however, the counterexample does not stand up to close inspection.

On his web site[3] Professor John McDonald of the University of Delaware displays drawings he made of mousetraps that contain fewer parts than the one I pictured in *Darwin's Black Box*. He asserts that the drawings show mousetraps need not have all the parts I pictured, thus the standard mousetrap is not irreducible. In defense of the mousetrap I will make a number of points, including (1) McDonald's reduced-component traps are not single-step intermediates in the building of the mousetrap I showed; (2) intelligence was intimately involved in constructing the series of traps; (3) if intelligence is necessary to make something as simple as a mousetrap, we have strong reason to think it is necessary to make the much more complicated machinery of the cell.

On his web site Professor McDonald was careful to make a critical distinction. He clearly stated "the reduced-complexity mousetraps . . . are intended to point out the logical flaw in the intelligent design argument; they're not intended as an analogy of how evolution works." The logical point Professor McDonald wished to make was that there are mousetraps that can work with fewer parts than the trap I pictured in my book. Let me say that I agree completely; in fact, I said so in my book (see the following extract). For example, one can dig a steep hole in the ground for mice to fall into and starve to death. Arguably, that has zero parts. One can catch mice with a glue trap, which has only one part. One can prop up a box with a stick, hoping a mouse will bump the stick and the box will fall on top of it. That has two parts. And so forth. There is no end to possible variation in mousetrap design. But, as I tried to emphasize in my book, the point that is relevant to Darwinian evolution is not whether one can make variant structures, but whether those structures lead, step-by-excruciatingly-tedious-Darwinian-step, to the structure I showed. I wrote:

> To feel the full force of the conclusion that a system is irreducibly complex and therefore has no functional precursors we need to distinguish between a physical precursor and a conceptual precursor. The trap described above is not the only system that can immobilize a mouse. On other occasions my family has used a glue trap. In theory at least, one can use a box propped open with a stick that could be tripped. Or one can simply shoot the mouse with a BB gun. However, these are not physical precursors to the standard mousetrap since they cannot be

transformed, step-by-Darwinian-step, into a trap with a base, hammer, spring, catch, and holding bar.[4]

As I agree with Professor McDonald that there could be mousetraps with fewer parts, the only relevant question is whether the mousetraps he drew are physical precursors, or merely conceptual precursors. Can they "be transformed, step-by-Darwinian-step" into the trap I pictured? No, they can't. To see why, let's examine his "one-piece" and "two-piece" traps. (To follow the discussion below it would be best to view McDonald's mousetraps on his web site.)

The single-piece trap, consisting of just a spring with extended arms, has one arm, under tension, propped up on the other arm. When a mouse jiggles it, the arm is released and comes down, pinning the mouse's paw against the other arm. Now, the first thing to notice is that the single-piece trap isn't a simple spring—it's got a very specific structure. If the lengths of the extended ends varied by much before their first bend, or if the angle of the bends differed somewhat, the trap wouldn't work. What's more, the strength of the material out of which the spring is made has to be consonant with the purpose of catching a mouse (for example, if it were made from an old Slinky it likely wouldn't work). It is not a simple starting point; it was intelligently selected. Nonetheless, I realize that in coming up with an analogy we have to start somewhere. So I will not complain about an intelligently selected starting point. However, the involvement of intelligence at any other point along the way invalidates the entire exercise as an analogy to a Darwinian process. Because Darwinism wholly rejects intelligent direction, Darwinists must agree that the involvement of intelligence at any point in a scenario (after the agreed-on starting point) is fatal. That point occurs immediately for our mousetrap.

The second mousetrap has a spring and a platform. One of the extended arms stands under tension at the very edge of the platform. The idea is that if a mouse in the vicinity jiggles the trap, the end of the arm slips over the edge and comes rushing down, and may pin the mouse's paw or tail against the platform. Now, the first thing to notice is that the arms of the spring are in a different relationship to each other than in the first trap. To get to the configuration of the spring in the second trap from the configuration in the first, it seems to me one would have to proceed through the following steps: (1) twist the arm that has one bend through about 90° so that the end segment is perpendicular to the axis of the spring and points toward the platform; (2) twist the other arm through about 180° so the first segment is pointing opposite to where it originally pointed (the exact value of the rotations depends on the lengths of the arms); (3) shorten one arm so that its length is less than the distance from the top of the platform to the floor (so that the end doesn't first hit the floor before pinning the mouse).[5] While the arms were being rotated and adjusted, the original one-piece trap would have lost function, and the second trap would not yet be working.

At this point we bring in a new piece, the platform, which is a simple piece of wood. One now has a spring resting on top of a platform. However, the spring cannot be under tension in this configuration unless it is fixed in place. It turns out that in the second mousetrap, not only has a platform been added, but two (barely visible) staples have been added as well. Thus we have gone not from a one-piece to a two-piece trap, but from a one- to a four-piece trap. Two staples are needed; if there were only one staple positioned as drawn, the tensed spring would be able to rotate out of position. The staples have to be positioned carefully with respect to the platform. They have to be arranged within a very narrow tolerance so that one arm of the spring teeters perilously on the edge of the platform or the trap doesn't work. If either of the staples is moved significantly from where it is drawn, the trap won't function. I should add that I did not emphasize the staples in my book because I was trying to make a simple point and didn't want to exhaust the readers with tedium. However, someone who wishes to seriously propose that the mousetrap I pictured is approachable in the tiny steps required by Darwinian processes would indeed have to deal with all the details, including the staples.

It is important to remember that the placement, size, shape, or any important feature (not just "piece") of a system can't just be chosen to fit the purposes of a person who wishes to simulate a Darwinian process. Rather, each significant feature has to be justified as being a small improvement. In the real world the occasional unselected feature might occur which serendipitously will be useful in the future, but invoking more than one unselected (neutral, nonadaptive) event in a Darwinian scenario seems to me impermissible because the improbability of the joint events starts to soar. In our current case the unselected event we are allowed was used up when we began with a special starting point.

I think the problems of rearranging the already-functioning first mousetrap shows the general difficulties one expects in trying to rearrange an already-functioning system into something else. The requirements ("selection pressures") that make a component suitable for one specialized system will generally make it unsuitable for another system without significant modification. Another problem we can note is that the second mousetrap is not an obvious improvement over the first; it is difficult to see how it would function any better than the one-piece trap. It's just that it's on the road to where we want to see the system end up—on the road to a distant target. That, of course, is intelligent direction.

The transition from the first to the second mousetrap is not analogous to a Darwinian process because (1) a number of separate steps are required to make the transition; (2) each step has to fall within a narrow range of tolerance to get to the target trap; and (3) function is lost until the transition is completed. In fact, the situation of going from the first trap to the second trap is best viewed not as a transition, but as building a different kind of trap using some old materials from the first trap (with major modifications) and some new materials. Far from being an analogy to a Darwinian process, the construction of the second trap is an example of intelligent design.

Horse Sense

I have to admit that even I find it tedious to discuss mousetraps in such excruciating detail. But the critical point is that this is exactly the level at which Darwinian evolution would have to work in the cell. Every relevant detail has to fit or the system fails. If an arm is too long or an angle not right or a staple placed incorrectly, the mouse dances free. If you want to get to a certain system, but the road there isn't a series of continual improvements, Darwinism won't take you there. It's important for those interested in these issues to realize that, when evaluating descriptive evolutionary scenarios (as opposed to experiments which I will discuss), one has to attend to the tiniest details (as I did here) to see if intelligence is directing the show. On the other hand, if one doesn't pay the strictest attention, Darwinian scenarios look much more plausible because one sees only the possibilities, not the problems. It's easy for a speaker to persuade an audience that the McDonald mousetraps represent a series of Darwinian intermediates on the way to a standard trap—that they show irreducible complexity is no big deal. All one has to do is gloss over the difficulties. But although our minds can skip over details, nature can't.

In the real world of biology the staples, bends, and so forth would be features of molecules, of proteins in particular. If two proteins don't bind each other in the correct orientation (aren't stapled right), if they aren't placed in the right positions, if their new activity isn't regulated correctly, if many details aren't exactly correct, then the putative Darwinian pathway is blocked. Now, it's hard, almost impossible, for persons without the appropriate science background to tell where such difficulties would occur in Darwinian scenarios for blood clotting or ciliary function or other biological systems. When they read Darwinian stories in a book or hear them in lectures, they generally have no independent information to judge the scenario. In such a situation one should ask oneself, "If a simple mousetrap requires intelligent design, what is the likelihood that the much more complicated molecular machines of the cell could be built step-by-tiny-Darwinian-step?" Keeping that question in mind will foster a healthy skepticism toward optimistic scenarios.

Why do the McDonald mousetraps look persuasive to some people? One reason for the persuasiveness of the example we can call the "Clever Hans effect." Clever Hans was the name of a horse who seemed to be pretty good at arithmetic. Its owner would give Hans a simple math problem such as 5 + 5, and the horse would stamp his hoof ten times, then stop. It eventually turned out that Clever Hans could pick up unconscious cues from its owner, who might raise his eyebrows or tilt his head when the horse's stamping reached the right value. The horse could even pick up unintentional cues from other people, not just the owner, who also apparently gave telltale reactions. In the case of Clever Hans, the human intelligence of the owner was inadvertently attributed to the horse. In my experience the same is invariably true of Darwinian scenarios—human intelligence is critical to guiding the scenario through difficulties toward the "proper" goal, but the intelligence is then attributed to natural selection. As with Clever Hans, the guidance is usually unconscious but is intelligent nonetheless.

Darwinian scenarios, either for building mousetraps or biochemical systems, are very easy to believe if we aren't willing or able to scrutinize the smallest details or to ask for experimental evidence. They invite us to admire the intelligence of natural selection. But the intelligence we are admiring is our own.

Notes

1. Charles Darwin, *The Origin of Species* 6th ed. (New York: New York University Press, 1988), 151.

2. Darwin, *The Origin of Species,* 154.

3. http://udel.edu/~mcdonald/mousetrap.html

4. M. J. Behe, *Darwin's Black Box: The Biochemical Challenge to Evolution* (New York: The Free Press, 1996), 43.

5. To play the game right, one has to compare the probability of these events happening with the probability of any slight "mutation" happening. To give a flavor of what that might mean, a mutation might involve bending the spring in the middle, changing the size of the platform, changing the tension on the spring, extending the end of a metal piece, and so on. A crude feel for the probabilities of the events can be obtained by examining the precision a feature must have for the trap to work. To get the probability for two or more unselected events (ones that don't improve the function), one multiplies the probabilities for each.

Chapter Eight

And the Wall Came Tumbling Down

POPE JOHN PAUL II AND THE COLLAPSE OF COMMUNISM

George Weigel

I would like to reflect on the historic impact of a man who believes that faith and freedom are intimately linked. Interestingly enough this man, who has had an immense impact on the history of our times, is neither a politician, a diplomat, nor an international relations theorist. That is, he does not wield power as the world conventionally understands "power." Rather, he is a pastor, an evangelist, and a witness to basic human rights. Pope John Paul II is convinced that ideas and moral convictions are levers with which to move the world. Ideas and values are distinctive forms of power. Reflecting on how the pope has exercised the power of truth is not only an interesting exercise in its own right; it may help us to understand how the world really works.

That John Paul II has had a considerable impact on contemporary history is now widely conceded by even his most implacable critics, inside and outside the Catholic Church. Yet one may well wonder whether those who think about the dynamics of history, professionally or as an avocation, have begun to come to grips intellectually with the meaning of John Paul II's accomplishment in the world of affairs—or with what that accomplishment

GEORGE WEIGEL is a Senior Fellow of the Ethics and Public Policy Center in Washington, where he holds the John M. Olin Chair in Religion and American Democracy. He is the author of the international best seller *Witness to Hope: The Biography of Pope John Paul II*, which is published in English by HarperCollins.

suggests about the working-out of history and the contours of world politics in the twenty-first century.

So my plan here is to sketch, briefly, the pope's accomplishment, as I have come to understand it as his biographer, using three examples; then I shall indicate, again briefly, some lessons from this accomplishment for the future; and finally, I shall suggest where the new intellectual terrain lies, post–John Paul II, for those interested in the impact of ideas and religiously grounded moral values on politics, especially the politics and ethics of international relations.

The Pope's Accomplishment

To understand John Paul II's concept of the dynamics of international relations—indeed, the dynamics of history itself—let's go back in our imaginations to the small Polish town of Wadowice, about forty miles southwest of Cracow, somewhere in the late 1920s. There, we meet a young Polish boy named Karol Wojtyla. Young Karol, we discover, has learned from his father, a retired military officer, and from his elementary and secondary schooling the great lesson of modern Polish history: that it was through its culture—its language, its literature, its religion—that Poland the nation survived when Poland the state was erased for 123 years from the map of Europe.

Between 1795, when the three great powers of East Central Europe—Prussia, Austria-Hungary, and Russia—completed the third and final partition of the Polish lands, and 1918, nothing labeled "Poland" appeared on any map of Europe. It was an unprecedented act of destruction, the vivisection of a historic, living state. Yet throughout those 123 years of wandering in the wilderness of history, the Polish nation survived because the idea of "Poland" survived. Indeed, it survived with such potency that the Polish nation could give birth to a new Polish state in the aftermath of World War I.

History viewed from the Vistula River basin looks different; it has a tangible spiritual dimension. Looking at history from that distinctive angle of vision, we learn that overwhelming material force can be resisted successfully through the resources of the human spirit—through culture. And in reflecting on that, we learn that culture—not politics, not economics, and not some combination of politics and economics—is the most dynamic, enduring factor in human affairs, at least over the long haul.

Having learned these lessons as a young man, Karol Wojtyla, a son of Poland whom the world would later know as Pope John Paul II, applied this concept of the priority of culture in history in resistance to the two great totalitarian powers that sought to subjugate Poland between 1939 and 1989.

He applied it in a variety of resistance activities against the draconian Nazi occupation of Poland from 1939 until 1945. The Nazis' strategic goal in Poland was to erase these Polish-Slavic *untermenschen* from the European New Order. One step toward achieving that goal was to decapitate the Polish nation by liquidating its intellectual, religious, and cultural leadership—thus, two months after Poland's defeat in September 1939, 186 professors from the Jagiellonian University were deported to the Sachsenhausen concentration camp. One effective means of resistance to this tactic of decapitation was to keep Polish culture alive. Karol Wojtyla was intensely involved in this, at the daily risk of his life, through his participation in a host of cultural resistance groups: the underground Jagiellonian University; clandestine literary, theatrical, and religious activities; a pioneering movement of civic renewal called UNIA which sought to lay the intellectual foundations for a postwar Christian democracy in Poland.

As a priest and bishop in Cracow from 1949 through 1978, Karol Wojtyla applied a similar "culture first" strategy to resistance against the communist effort to rewrite Poland's history and redefine Poland's culture. Wojtyla had no direct "political" involvement over those three gray decades. He could have cared less about the internal politics of the Polish communist party, who was up and who was down in the politburo, the twists and turns of the official party line. But his efforts to nurture an informed, intelligent Catholic laity were examples of what a later generation of democratic activists would call "building civil society"—and thus laying the groundwork for an active resistance movement with political traction.

Pope John Paul II has applied this strategy of culturally driven change on a global stage since his election on October 16, 1978.

In 1992, when Oxford University Press published my study *The Final Revolution: The Resistance Church and the Collapse of Communism,* there were many eyebrows raised within the professoriate and the punditocracy about my claim that the church and the pope had played pivotal roles in the collapse of European communism. When I amplified that claim in *Witness to Hope: The Biography of Pope John Paul II,* which was published seven years later, no one batted an eye. Over the course of the 1990s, John Paul II's crucial role in the collapse of European communism came to be generally recognized—even by Mikhail Gorbachev, who might have been expected to take a somewhat rueful view of the matter. But while the pope's pivotal role in these epic events is now recognized, it does not seem well-understood.

John Paul II was not, *pace* Tad Szulc in his biography of the pope, a wily diplomat skillfully negotiating a transition beyond one-party rule in Poland. He was not, *pace* Carl Bernstein and Marco Politi in their fantasy-biography *His Holiness,* a co-conspirator with Ronald Reagan in a "holy alliance" to effect communism's demise. He was not, *pace* the late Jonathan Kwitny in his lengthy study of Wojtyla's career, a Gandhi in a white cassock running a nonviolent resistance movement in Poland through a clandestine messenger service from the Vatican.

Rather, John Paul II shaped the politics of East Central Europe in the 1980s as a pastor, an evangelist, and a witness to basic human rights. Primary-source evidence for this is found in the texts of the pope's epic June 1979 pilgrimage to his homeland, nine days on which the history of the twentieth century pivoted. In some forty sermons, addresses, lectures, and impromptu remarks, the pope told his fellow countrymen, in so many words: "You are not who they say you are. Let me remind you who you are." By restoring to the Polish people their authentic history and culture—by giving back to his people their identity—John Paul II created a revolution of conscience that, fourteen months later, produced the nonviolent Solidarity resistance movement, a unique hybrid of workers and intellectuals: a "forest planed by aroused consciences," as the pope's friend, the philosopher Józef Tischner, once put it. And by restoring to his people a form of freedom and a fearlessness that communism could not reach, John Paul II set in motion the human dynamics that eventually led, over a decade, to what we know as the Revolution of 1989.

Those nine days in June 1979 were not only a time of catharsis for a people long frustrated by their inability to express the truth about themselves publicly. Together, they also formed one decisive, historic moment in which convictions were crystallized, to the point where the mute acquiescence that, as Václav Havel wrote, made continuing communist rule possible was shattered. Many people had long wanted to say "No" to communism. But they could not do so, publicly, except on the basis of a higher and more compelling "Yes." Providing that "Yes" was what John Paul II did in June 1979. Moreover, it was not simply that, as French historian Alain Besancon nicely put it, "people regained the private ownership of their tongues" during the Solidarity revolution. It was what those tongues said—their new willingness to defy what Havel called the communist "culture of the lie"—that made the crucial difference.

To be sure, there were other factors in creating the Revolution of 1989: the policies of Ronald Reagan, Margaret Thatcher, and Helmut Kohl; Mikhail Gorbachev, a Soviet leader not formed in the brutalities of Stalin's purge trials; the human rights provisions of the Helsinki Final Act and their effects throughout Europe and in linking human rights activists in the captive nations and the old democracies. But if we ask why communism collapsed when it did—in 1989 rather than 1999 or 2009 or 2019—and how it did—without mass violence (with the sole exception of Romania)—then sufficient account has to be taken of June 1979 and the revolution of conscience it ignited. This was a different kind of revolution, because the revolutionaries were a different sort of people—people who understood, as Adam Michnik aptly put it, that "those who begin by tearing down Bastilles end up building their own."

This singular contribution of the pope in June 1979 is a point stressed by local witnesses. When I first began researching *The Final Revolution* in 1990, I thought that the church and the pope had had something to do with the Revolution of 1989. In talking with dozens, even hundreds, of the people of the revolution, however, I came to a different, more expansive view. Poles, Czechs, and Slovaks, religious and secular alike, were unanimous in their testimony about the crucial impact of June 1979, which had launched a different kind of revolution—a revolution of conscience that made a nonviolent political revolution possible. June 1979, they unanimously insisted, was when "1989" started.

(Parenthetically, it's worth noting that the West largely missed this. Thus the *New York Times* editorial of June 5, 1979: "As much as the visit of Pope John Paul II to Poland must reinvigorate and reinspire the Roman Catholic Church in Poland, it does not threaten the political order of the nation or of Eastern Europe." But two other Slavic readers of the signs of the times were not at all confused: Alexander Solzhenitsyn and Yuri Andropov both knew that the rise of John Paul II and the deployment of his "culture first" strategy of social change were a profound threat to the Soviet order. The degree of seriousness with which Andropov took this threat may be inferred from the events in St. Peter's Square on May 13, 1981, when Mehmet Ali Agca tried to assassinate Pope John Paul II.)

"1989" had certain unique, unrepeatable characteristics, like any great historical event. Still, John Paul II applied a similar strategy—the renovation of political life through the restoration of public moral culture—when he went to Chile in 1987. Fourteen years of the Pinochet government, following the crisis of the Allende regime, had created deep divisions in Chilean society. There were raw wounds in the body politic because of human rights abuses and the recalcitrance of the left; there was, in a phrase, no "civil society," and that lack made a transition to a democratic future impossible.

Therefore, John Paul II, in collaboration with the Chilean bishops, decided that the public purpose of his 1987 pilgrimage to Chile would be to help reconstitute civil society through a reclamation of Chile's Christian culture. The great theme for the visit would be that "Chile's vocation is for understanding, not confrontation." The papal pilgrimage would, as one of its organizers put it to me, "take back the streets," which had been places of fear under Allende and Pinochet, and transform them once again into places of community. And people would be deliberately mixed together at the venues for the papal masses: Chileans would be compelled, under the eye of their common religious "father," to look at each other once again as persons rather than ideological objects. And it seems no accident that, some eighteen months after the papal visit had accelerated the process of reconstructing Chilean civil society, a national plebiscite voted to move beyond military rule and restore democracy.

The third example of John Paul II's "culture first" approach to political change can be found in his pilgrimage to Cuba in January 1998. There, the pope did not mention once the current Cuban regime—not once in five days. Rather, he re-read Cuban history through the lens of a Christianity that had formed a distinctively Cuban people from native peoples, Spaniards, and Black African slaves. And he re-read the Cuban national liberation struggle of the nineteenth century through the prism of its Christian inspiration. Here, as in Poland in 1979, the pope was restoring to a people their authentic history and culture. In doing so, he was also calling for a reinsertion of Cuba into history and into the hemisphere, asking the Cuban people to stop thinking of themselves as victims (the theme of Fidel Castro's welcoming address), and to start thinking of themselves as the protagonists of their own destiny.

Lessons Learned

Several lessons can be drawn from reflecting on the distinctive impact of Pope John Paul II on the history of our times.

First, the experience of John Paul II suggests that what we call "civil society" is not simply institutional: a free press, free trade unions, free business organizations, free associations, and so forth. Civil society has an essential moral core. Civil society is built on the foundation of common moral convictions about the nature of the human person and the requirements of human community.

Second, John Paul II's "culture first" strategy reminds us that "power" cannot be measured solely in terms of aggregates of military or economic capability. The "power of the powerless" is a real form of power. Moral conviction, deployed in such a way as to restore to peoples their authentic identity, can be an Archimedean lever from which to move the world.

In the third place, the pope's impact demonstrates that non-state actors count in contemporary world politics, sometimes in decisive ways. John Paul II did not shape the history of our times as the temporal sovereign of the Vatican City microstate, but as the bishop of Rome and the universal pastor of the Catholic Church. At the end of a century which began with secular modernity convinced that human beings would quickly "outgrow" their "need" for religion, one of the most potent actors on the world stage was the holder of the world's oldest religious office. The world does not work the way the world sometimes thinks it works—or the way conventional academic analyses of the dynamics of history and politics tell us it works.

The Work Remaining

Still, for all its "worldly" accomplishments, the pontificate of John Paul II has left some gaps in our understanding that urgently need filling in the years just ahead.

It is curious that this son of a soldier, who has expressed his respect for the military vocation on many occasions, has not developed the Catholic

Church's just war doctrine. This was most evident during the Gulf War, but beyond such relatively conventional conflicts there are new issues today at the intersection of ethics and world politics—the problem of outlaw states, the morality of preemption in the face of weapons of mass destruction, the locus of "legitimate authority" in the international community—that the pope has simply not addressed. Others must take up that task.

The same can be said for "humanitarian intervention," which the pope identified as a "moral duty" in an address to the U.N.'s Food and Agricultural Organization in 1992. But this "duty" was not defined. On whom does it fall, and why? By what means is it to be discharged? What about the claims of sovereignty? These are large questions that demand the most careful reflection.

The Irony of Success

John Paul II has been the most politically consequential pope in centuries. But his impact did not come through the normal modalities of politics. He had no army. His success did not, in the main, come through the normal instruments of diplomacy. In terms of the history of ideas, his "culture first" reading of history is a sharp challenge to the regnant notions that politics runs history, or economics runs history. Does the fact of the pope's success suggest that we are moving into a period in which nation-states are of less consequence in "world affairs"? Or were the accomplishments I've outlined here idiosyncratic, the result of a singular personality meeting a unique set of circumstances with singular prescience and effect? There is much to chew on here, for students of history and international affairs, in the years immediately ahead. But that we have been living, in this pontificate, through the days of a giant seems clear enough.

Selected Bibliography

Ahlstrom, Sidney E., ed. *Theology in America: The Major Protestant Voices from Puritanism to Neo-Orthodoxy.* Indianapolis, Ind: Bobbs-Merrill, 1967.

Alley, Robert S. *So Help Me God: Religion and the Presidency: Wilson to Nixon.* Richmond, Va: John Knox Press, 1972.

Allitt, Patrick. *Catholic Intellectuals and Conservative Politics in America, 1950–1985.* Ithaca, N.Y.: Cornell University Press, 1993.

Anderson, Charles H. *White Protestant Americans: From National Origins to Religious Group.* Englewood Cliffs, N.J.: Prentice Hall, 1970.

Atkins, Stanley, and Theodore McConnell, eds. *Churches on the Wrong Side.* Chicago: Regnery, 1986.

Bainton, Roland. *The Reformation of the Sixteenth Century.* Boston: Beacon Press, 1952.

Barton, David. *The Bulletproof George Washington: An Account of God's Providential Care.* Houston, Tex: Wallbuilders Press, 1990.

———. *Original Intent: The Courts, the Constitution and Religion.* Houston, Tex: Wallbuilders Press, 1997.

Behe, Michael J. *Darwin's Black Box: The Biochemical Challenge to Evolution.* New York: Simon & Schuster, 1998.

Bellah, Robert N. *On Morality and Society.* Chicago: University of Chicago Press, 1973.

———. *The Broken Covenant.* New York: Seabury, 1975.

Bellah, Robert N., and Phillip E. Hammond. *Varieties of Civil Religion.* New York: Harper & Row, 1982.

Benson, Peter L. *Religion on Capitol Hill.* New York: Harper & Row, 1982.

Berger, Peter L. *The Sacred Canopy.* Garden City, N.Y.: Doubleday, 1967.

————. *A Rumor of Angels*. Garden City, N.Y.: Doubleday, 1970.

Berger, Peter L., and Richard J. Neuhaus. *Movement and Revolution: On American Radicalism*. New York: Anchor, 1970.

————. *To Empower the People: The Role of Mediating Structures in Public Policy*. Washington, D.C.: American Enterprise Institute, 1977.

Billington, James M. *Icon and the Axe*. New York: Knopf, 1989.

————. *Fire in the Minds of Men: Origins of the Revolutionary Faith*. Somerset, N.J.: Transaction, 1998.

Brown, Harold O. J. *The Reconstruction of the Republic: A Modern Theory of the State 'Under God' and Its Political, Social and Economic Structures*. Washington, D.C.: Arlington House, 1977.

————. *Heresies: The Image of Christ in the Mirror of Heresy and Orthodoxy: From the Apostles to the Present*. Garden City, N.Y.: Doubleday, 1984.

Carroll, Peter N., ed. *Religion and the Coming of the American Revolution*. Waltham, Mass: Ginn-Blaisdell, 1970.

Carter, Stephen L. *The Culture of Disbelief: How American Law and Politics Trivialize Religious Devotion*. New York: Doubleday, 1994.

————. *The Dissent of the Governed: A Meditation on Law, Religion, and Loyalty*. Cambridge: Harvard University Press, 1999a.

————. *Manners, Morals, and the Etiquette of Democracy*. New York: Harper, 1999b.

————. *God's Name in Vain: The Wrongs and Rights of Religion in Politics*. New York: Basic Books, 2001.

Chadwick, Owen. *The Reformation*. New York: Penguin, 1964.

Cherry, Conrad, ed. *God's New Israel: Religious Interpretations of American Destiny*. Englewood Cliffs, N.J.: Prentice Hall, 1971.

Conkin, Paul K. *When All the Gods Trembled: Darwinism, Scopes, and American Intellectuals*. Lanham, Md: Rowman & Littlefield, 2001.

Douglas, R. Bruce, and Joshua Mitchell, eds. *A Nation under God?* Lanham, Md.: Rowman & Littlefield, 2000.

Dreisbach, Daniel A. *Real Threat and Mere Shadow*. Wheaton, Ill.: Crossway, 1987.

————. *Religion and Politics in the Early Republic*. Lexington, Ky.: University of Kentucky Press, 1996.

————. *Thomas Jefferson and the Wall of Separation Between Church and State*. New York: New York University Press, 2002.

Dunn, Charles W. *American Political Theology*. New York: Praeger, 1984.

————, ed. *Religion in American Politics*. Washington, D.C.: Congressional Quarterly Press, 1989.

————. *The Scarlet Thread of Scandal: Morality and the American Presidency.* Lanham, Md.: Rowman & Littlefield, 2001.

————. *The Conservative Tradition in America.* Lanham, Md.: Rowman & Littlefield, rev. ed., 2003.

Durham, Martin. *The Christian Right, the Far Right and the Boundaries of American Conservatism.* New York: Manchester University Press, 2001.

Eidsmoe, John. *Christianity and the Constitution.* Grand Rapids, Mich.: Baker Books, 1987.

Elazar, Daniel. *The Covenant Connection: From Federal Theology to Modern Federalism.* Lanham, Md.: Lexington Books, 2000.

Eliot, T. S. *Christianity and Culture.* New York: Harcourt, Brace & World, 1968.

Elshtain, Jean Bethke, ed. *Democracy on Trial.* New York: Basic Books, 1995.

————. *Augustine and the Limits of Politics.* Notre Dame, Ind.: University of Notre Dame Press, 1998.

————. *The Necessity of Politics: Reclaiming American Public Life.* Chicago: University of Chicago Press, 2000a.

————. *Who Are We? Critical Reflections and Hopeful Possibilities.* Grand Rapids, Mich.: Eerdmans, 2000b.

Evans, M. Stanton. *The Theme Is Freedom.* Washington, D.C.: Regnery Publishing, 1994.

Formicola, Jo Renee, and Hubert Morken. *Religious Leaders and Faith-Based Politics.* Lanham, Md.: Rowman & Littlefield, 2001.

Fowler, Robert Booth. *Religion and Politics in America.* Metuchen, N.J.: American Theological Association, 1985.

————. *Unconventional Partners.* Grand Rapids, Mich.: Eerdmans, 1989.

————. *The Dance with Community.* Lawrence, Kan.: University Press of Kansas, 1994.

George, Robert P. *Making Men Moral: Civil Liberties and Public Morality.* New York: Oxford University Press, 1995.

————. *In Defense of Natural Law.* New York: Oxford University Press, 2000.

————. *The Clash of Orthodoxies: Law, Religion, and Morality in Crisis.* Wilmington, Del.: ISI Books, 2001.

Goldberg, George. *Church, State and the Constitution.* Chicago: Regnery, 1987.

Gregg, Gary L. *Vital Remnants: America's Founding and the Western Tradition.* Wilmington, Del.: ISI Books, 1999.

Hancock, Ralph Cornell. *Calvin and the Foundations of Modern Politics.* Ithaca, N.Y.: Cornell University Press, 1989.

Hanna, Mary. *Catholics and American Politics*. Cambridge, Mass.: Harvard University Press, 1979.

Hart, Benjamin. *Faith and Freedom*. Dallas, Tex.: Lewis & Stanley, 1988.

Heineman, Kenneth J. *God Is a Conservative: Religion, Politics, and Morality in Contemporary America*. New York: New York University Press, 1998.

Herberg, Will. *Protestant, Catholic, Jew*. Garden City, N.Y.: Doubleday Anchor, 1960.

Hitchcock, James. *Catholicism and Modernity*. New York: Seabury Press, 1979.

Hollowell, John. *The Moral Foundations of Democracy*. Chicago: University of Chicago Press, 1954.

Hudson, Winthrop S., ed. *Nationalism and Religion in America: Concepts of American Identity and Mission*. New York: Harper & Row, 1970.

Hunter, James Davison. *Culture Wars: The Struggle to Define America*. New York: Basic Books, 1991.

Hutson, James H., ed. *Religion and the Founding of the American Republic*. Washington, D.C.: Library of Congress, 1998.

———. *Religion and the New Republic*. Lanham, Md.: Rowman & Littlefield, 1999.

Jaki, Stanley L. *Cosmos and Creator*. Chicago: Regnery, 1982.

———. *The Savior of Science*. Chicago: Regnery, 1987.

———. *The Only Chaos and Other Essays*. Bryn Mawr, Penn.: Intercollegiate Studies Associates Press, 1990.

———. *Patterns and Principles and Other Essays*. Bryn Mawr, Penn.: Intercollegiate Studies Associates Press, 1995.

Kelley, Dean M. *Why Conservative Churches Are Growing*. New York: Harper & Row, 1972.

Kemeny, Paul Charles. *Princeton in the Nation's Service: Religious Ideals and Educational Practice, 1868–1928*. New York: Oxford, 1998.

Kilpatrick, William K. *Psychological Seduction: The Failure of Modern Psychology*. Nashville, Tenn.: Thomas Nelson, 1983.

Kraynak, Robert P. *Christian Faith and Modern Democracy: God and Politics in the Fallen World*. Notre Dame, Ind.: University of Notre Dame Press, 2001.

Lawler, Philip F. *The Ultimate Weapon*. Chicago: Regnery, 1984.

———. *Postmodernism Rightly Understood*. Lanham, Md.: Rowman & Littlefield, 1999.

Lefever, Ernest W. *Amsterdam to Nairobi: The World Council of Churches and the Third World*. Washington, D.C.: Ethics and Public Policy Center, 1979.

Lewis, C. S. *Mere Christianity.* New York: Macmillan, 1960.

———. *The Abolition of Man.* New York: Macmillan, 1965.

———. *God in the Dock: Essays on Theology and Ethics.* Grand Rapids, Mich.: Eerdmans, 1970.

Lugg, Catherine A. *For God and Country: Conservatism and American School Policy.* New York: Peter Lang, 1996.

Marsden, George. *Fundamentalism in American Culture.* New York: Oxford University Press, 1980.

———. *The Soul of the American University: From Protestant Establishment to Established Nonbelief.* New York: Oxford University Press, 1996.

———. *The Outrageous Idea of Christian Scholarship.* New York: Oxford University Press, 1998.

Marty, Martin. *Pilgrims in Their Own Land.* New York: Penguin Books, 1984.

McLoughlin, William G. *Revivals, Awakenings and Reform.* Chicago: University of Chicago Press, 1978.

Muggeridge, Malcolm. *Jesus Rediscovered.* Garden City, N.Y.: Doubleday, 1969.

———. *Christ and the Media.* Grand Rapids, Mich.: Eerdmans, 1977.

Nash, Ronald H. *Social Justice and the Christian Church.* Milford, Mich.: Mott Media, 1983.

———, ed. *Liberation Theology.* Milford, Mich.: Mott Media, 1984.

Niebuhr, H. Richard. *The Church Against the World.* New York: Willett Clark, 1935.

Niebuhr, Reinhold. *Moral Man and Immoral Society.* New York: Scribner's, 1932, 1960.

———. *The Irony of American History.* New York: Scribner's, 1952.

———. *Christian Realism and Political Problems.* New York: Kelley, 1953.

———. *The Self and the Dramas of History.* New York: Scribner's, 1955.

———. *The Children of Light and the Children of Darkness.* New York: Scribner's, 1960.

———. *Christianity and Power Politics.* New York: Anchor, 1969.

Neuhaus, Richard John. *The Naked Public Square.* Grand Rapids, Mich.: Eerdmans, 1984.

Noll, Mark A., ed. *Religion and American Politics.* New York: Oxford University Press, 1989.

———. *The Scandal of the Evangelical Mind.* Grand Rapids, Mich.: Eerdmans, 1996.

———. *The Old Religion in a New World: The History of North American Christianity.* Grand Rapids, Mich.: Eerdmans, 2001.

————. *The Search for Christian America.* Colorado Springs, Col.: 1989.

Novak, Michael. *The Spirit of Democratic Capitalism.* New York: Simon & Schuster, 1982.

————. *Freedom with Justice: Catholic Social Thought and Liberal Institutions.* San Francisco: Harper & Row, 1984.

————. *On Two Wings: Humble Faith and Common Sense at the American Founding.* San Francisco: Encounter Books, 2001.

O'Donovan, Joan Lockwood, and Oliver O'Donovan, eds. *From Irenaeus to Grotius: A Sourcebook in Christian Political Thought 100–1625.* Grand Rapids, Mich.: William B. Eerdmans Pub. Co., 1999.

Olasky, Marvin. *Prodigal Press: The Anti-Christian Bias of the American News Media.* Wheaton, Ill.: 1988.

————. *The Tragedy of American Compassion.* Washington: Regnery, 1995.

————. *Fighting for Liberty and Virtue: Political and Cultural Wars in Eighteenth-Century America.* Washington: Regnery, 1996.

————. *Compassionate Conservatism.* New York: Free Press, 2000.

Parrington, Vernon L. *Main Currents in American Thought.* New York: Simon & Schuster, 1982.

Penchansky, David. *The Politics of Biblical Theology: A Postmodern Reading.* Macon, Ga.: Mercer University Press, 1998.

Rauschenbusch, Walter. *A Theology for the Social Gospel.* New York: Macmillan, 1917.

Reichley, A. James. *Religion in American Public Life.* Washington, D.C.: Brookings Institution, 1985.

————. *Faith in Politics.* Washington, D.D.: Brookings Institution, 2002.

————. *The Values Connection.* Lanham, Md.: Rowman & Littlefield, 2001.

Rice, Charles W. *Beyond Abortion: The Theory and Practice of the Secular State.* Chicago: Franciscan Herald Press, 1978.

Schaeffer, Francis A. *The Complete Works of Francis Schaeffer.* Westchester, Ill.: Crossway Books, 1985.

Schall, James V. *Liberation Theology.* San Francisco: Ignatius Press, 1982.

————. *The Politics of Heaven and Hell.* Lanham, Md.: University Press of America, 1984.

————, ed. *Out of Justice, Peace and Winning the Peace.* San Francisco: Ignatius Press, 1984.

Scully, Michael. *The Best of This World.* Lanham, Md.: University Press of America, 1986.

Segers, Mary A., ed. *Piety, Politics, and Pluralism.* Lanham, Md.: Rowman & Littlefield, 2001.

Sheldon, Garrett Ward, and Daniel A. Dreisbach. *Religion and Political Culture in Jefferson's Virginia.* Lanham, Md.: Rowman & Littlefield, 2000.

Singer, Gregg. *A Theological Interpretation of American History.* Philadelphia: Presbyterian and Reformed Publishing Co., 1964.

Solzhenitsyn, Alexander I. *A World Split Apart.* New York: Harper & Row, 1978.

Stanmeyer, William. *Clear and Present Danger.* Ann Arbor, Mich.: Servant Press, 1983.

Stevenson, William R. *Sovereign Grace: The Place and Significance of Christian Freedom in John Calvin's Political Thought.* New York: Oxford University Press, 1999.

Thomas, Cal, and Ed Dobson. *Blinded by Might: Can the Religious Right Save America?* New York: Harper-Collins, 1999.

Tinder, Glenn. *The Political Meaning of Christianity.* Baton Rouge, La.: LSU Press, 1989.

Vitz, Paul C. *Psychology as Religion: The Cult of Self-Worship.* Grand Rapids, Mich.: Eerdmans, 1977.

Wald, Ken. *Religion and Politics in the United States.* Washington, D.C.: CQ Press, 1996.

Weaver, Mary J., and R. Scott Appleby, eds. *Being Right: Conservative Catholics in America.* Bloomington, Ind.: Indiana University Press, 1995.

Weigel, George. *Century of Catholic Social Thought.* Lanham, Md.: University Press of America, 1991.

―――. *Soul of the World: Notes on the Future of Public Catholicism.* Grand Rapids, Mich.: Eerdmans, 1996.

―――. *Witness to Hope: The Biography of John Paul II.* New York: Harper, 2001.

West, Thomas G. *Vindicating the Founders.* Lanham, Md.: Rowman & Littlefield, 2001.

Wilcox, Clyde. *Onward Christian Soldiers? The Religious Right in American Politics.* Boulder, Col.: Westview Press, 1996.

Wuthnow, Robert. *The Restructuring of American Religion.* Princeton, N.J.: Princeton University Press, 1988.